ENESCO®

Then and Now

An Unauthorized Collector's Guide

Kathleen Deel

Schiffer Publishing Ltd®

4880 Lower Valley Road, Atglen, PA 19310 USA

Dedication

This price guide is dedicated to the memory of my beloved husband of forty-five years who went to join his heavenly Father as this book was nearing completion. We greatly miss his presence among us, but how great must be his reward in heaven. To all the families out there who know the heartbreak of a loved one struggling with this terrible disease known as congestive heart failure, my prayers are with you.

Library of Congress Control Number: 2001091789

Designed by John P. Cheek
Cover design by Bruce M. Waters
Type set in Americana XBd BT/Zurich BT

ISBN: 0-7643-1453-X
Printed in China
1 2 3 4

Published by Schiffer Publishing Ltd.
4880 Lower Valley Road
Atglen, PA 19310
Phone: (610) 593-1777; Fax: (610) 593-2002
E-mail: Schifferbk@aol.com
Please visit our web site catalog at
www.schifferbooks.com
We are always looking for people to write books on new and related subjects. If you have an idea for a book, please contact us at the above address.

This book may be purchased from the publisher.
Include $3.95 for shipping.
Please try your bookstore first.
You may write for a free catalog.

In Europe, Schiffer books are distributed by
Bushwood Books
6 Marksbury Avenue
Kew Gardens
Surrey TW9 4JF England
Phone: 44 (0) 20 8392 8585
Fax: 44 (0) 20 8392 9876
E-mail: Bushwd@aol.com
Free postage in the UK. Europe: air mail at cost.

Contents

Acknowledgments

A price guide such as this is never a one man operation and this book is no exception. Without the help of my collecting friends this book would never have come into being. First and foremost, my heartfelt thanks to Denise Dittner, who not only took pictures of her own and her children's collections, but also traveled to other states to photograph her mother's and cousin's collections. Not only did she supply pictures, but constantly searched the Internet for unusual Enesco items to aid me in my research. My good friend, Ruth Worthington, supplied, as usual, wonderful photos of her fabulous head vase collection. Thank you, Ruth, for being such a good friend and supporter for so many years. My friend, Jean Payne, along with her collecting family, daughter Donna Weddle and granddaughter Tammy Nash, supplied many pictures of their various collections, adding greatly to the diversity of this guide. Dee Thompson was kind enough to supply me with some great pictures of her lady planter collection and to lend her moral support and encouragement. Thank you Dee, for just being you. My daughter, Kim Lambert, made her collections available for my ever present camera and Mary O'Malley supplied me with photos of some of her choice Enesco items. Thank you one and all for your love and support, it made my task so much easier.

Introduction

Enesco is one of the oldest importing companies in the United States, dating back to 1888, when it was known as the N. Shure Company. A 1954 catalog places the N. Shure Company at 200 West Adams Street in Chicago, Illinois, with a line of giftware, novelty items, and kitchenware imported from Japan. Their showrooms were located in Chicago but gift shows were held throughout an area that included Wisconsin, Minnesota, Nebraska, Ohio, Kansas, Missouri, and Indiana. In addition to a general catalog, they also distributed furniture and sporting goods catalogs designed as counter catalogs so customers could make their own selections.

In 1958, Eugene Freedman joined the company as a salesman, and was later to become its President and CEO. A 1958 catalog shows a name change to Enesco Imports, a division of N. Shure Company. The N and S were taken from N. Shure and thus was created the new name, Enesco. The 1958 catalog was not a large one, but contained some lines which have become present day collectibles, most notably Humpty Dumpty, Kitchen Pixie, and Sweet Shoppe. A 1965 catalog was somewhat larger and pictured a line called Mother-in-the-Kitchen, which was destined to become a very desirable collectible some thirty years later. In addition, Dearie is Weary and Busy Biddy made their appearance at this time, as well as some great head vases and lady planters. The first sign of diversification in origin of imports appeared with the addition of glass from Italy and Portugal, ceramic items from Spain, as well as imports from Japan, Taiwan, the Philippines, and Hong Kong.

The late 1960s and 1970s were difficult times for importing companies, as their source for cheap ceramic items from Japan dried up due to that country's transformation into a major exporter of automobiles and electronic items. Enesco had already begun to look for new sources of supply as evidenced in the 1965 catalog, and while other major importing companies went out of business, Enesco not only survived, but prospered, due to innovative management. By 1980, a greatly expanded catalog was produced, reflecting a change of address to Elk Grove Village, just outside Chicago, with Eugene Freedman as President of Enesco Imports Corporation. The catalog contained a great variety of items, including Oriental giftware, Art Nouveau gifts, musicals, crystal, capodimonte and majolica, oxolyte and alabaster giftware, Italian figurines, thimbles and thimble boxes, wall decor, wood and brass items, kitchenware, baby and religious gifts, as well as plush toys and personalized items. More importantly, the beginning of what was to become a huge stepping stone to Enesco's future success made its first appearance. Collectible lines featuring talented designers, such as Suzy Spofford, Lucy Rigg, Eve Rockwell, and Kersten Brothers were prominently displayed. Importing countries included Italy, Taiwan, and Sri Lanka, as well as Japan. Enesco's sales offices had expanded to include the whole country, reaching from New York City to Miami to Los Angeles. Precious Moments made its first small beginning in 1978 and by the 1980s Enesco was on its way to becoming one of the top importing companies in the United States.

Throughout the 1980s and 1990s, clever marketing propelled Enesco into the giant that it is today. Designers were licensed to produce their designs for Enesco, and collector's clubs, newsletters, certificates of adoption, and the practice of retiring pieces after a limited production run were all designed to make an item more desirable and thus more salable. The boxes produced especially for each line were works of art in themselves, reminiscent of how the Avon Company boosted sales through clever packaging.

In 1983, Enesco was sold to Stanhome, Inc., a company based in Massachusetts. The company's first operation overseas, Enesco International, Ltd., began in 1985, and the Enesco Worldwide Giftware Group was created in 1988 to include Enesco Corporation and its operations throughout the world.

The Precious Moments line was instrumental in turning "Enesco" into a household word, and, in fact, many people think that Enesco actually came into being at the time the Precious Moments line was introduced. It has been their most successful and best known line, and probably the longest running, still going strong after more than twenty years. It is followed by Cherished Teddies, designed by Lucy Rigg, depicting lovable teddy bears doing people things. Enesco's lines now include more than ten thousand gift, collectible, and decorative items. In

1994, Enesco's Home Gallery was created, featuring high quality collectibles and home furnishing products.

Today, Enesco's corporate offices are located in Itasca, Illinois, with subsidiaries in Canada, Great Britain, Germany, France, and Hong Kong. They employ more than 1,600 administrative personnel in eighteen locations throughout the world and their sales force numbers 185. Their showroom, warehouse, and distribution facility are still located in Elk Grove Village.

Along with its extraordinary growth, Enesco is known for its dedication to charitable giving. Its Precious Moments line emphasizes religious values, while its many product lines featuring endearing animal figurines are instrumental in teaching children, as well as adults, to love and cherish our four legged friends. The Enesco Company is a shining example of how good management and innovative marketing ideas can turn a small importing company into a corporate giant.

A Word About Pricing

This price guide is a comprehensive look at all of Enesco's imports from the 1950s through the 1990s. Of course it would be impossible to show all of the company's present lines—that is not within the scope of this book. It is also not intended to compete with any other price guides issued on a regular basis that cover only one particular line or a small group of lines. It is intended to inform collectors of the price at which a collectible is currently selling on the open market, yet is not positive proof of what you can expect to obtain if you should decide to part with some of your treasures.

Pricing for Enesco pieces from the 1950s through the 1980s is not difficult. They sell in a predictable range on the Internet, depending on scarcity, desirability, and condition. Items issued in the 1990s are more difficult to price, not because of a lack of information regarding their selling price, but because the prices shown in this price guide may not meet a collector's expectations. Most collectors buy what they buy because they like the item, not because they are looking for a great appreciation in value. Some of the items in the 1990s section have increased in value, but many are selling for only a fraction of their original purchase price. Many lines were not successful and were of short duration, becoming less than desirable on the secondary market and priced accordingly.

The actual selling price of a collectible depends on who views the item as desirable, how scarce it is, and above all, what condition it is in. If your item is greatly in demand, not easy to find, and in mint condition, you can expect to receive top dollar for it. If your item is not particularly desirable in the eyes of collectors, if there is a glut on the market, or if it is in poor condition, you may have difficulty selling it.

There are over seven thousand listings for Enesco items at any given time on the eBay online auction site. Some listings contain multiple items, so it is safe to say that upwards of ten thousand Enesco pieces are advertised for sale on a daily basis on this site. Many auctions close without any bids but the more desirable items sell quickly at very gratifying prices to their owners. Prices shown in this guide have been compiled over the period of one year from Internet auction sales and reflect the average selling price, omitting the high spikes which can occur when a very desirable item is first put on the market and a bidding war erupts. After the first sale at a very high price, other sellers decide to market a similar item and the initial inflated selling price is never again met. This price guide is based on the average selling price of an item over an extended period of time and is only a guide. As always, it is up to the individual to determine what he or she is willing to pay for any given item.

Chapter One
1950s and 1960s

Beaver Dam

A very collectible line, pieces of "Beaver Dam" sell quickly on the Internet. Supply seems to be limited, so prices are on the high side. There are salt and pepper shakers, a teapot, spoon rest, and mustard, ketchup, and jelly containers. Other pieces may be found. The red and gold Enesco Japan label indicates this line probably dates from the early 1960s.

Spoon Rest, 5.75", red and gold Enesco Japan label, $18-20

Salt and Pepper Shakers, 3.25", no mark, $18-20

Teapot, 7", red and gold Enesco Japan label, $40-45

Mustard Container, 4.5", no mark, $25-30

Ketchup Container, 4.5", no mark, $25-30

Beaver Dam Collection

Birthday Sets

Birthday sets, which can include days of the week as well as months of the year, are very popular with collectors. The early birthday sets consisted mainly of angels, both boys and girls; later sets consisted of children and even animals. The boy angel sets are scarcer and usually command a higher price.

January Angel, 3.25", E-2827, $18-20

March Angel, 3.25", E-2827, $18-20

October Angel, 3.25", E-2827, $18-20

February Angel, 3.25", E-2827, $18-20

August Angel, 3.25", E-2827, $18-20

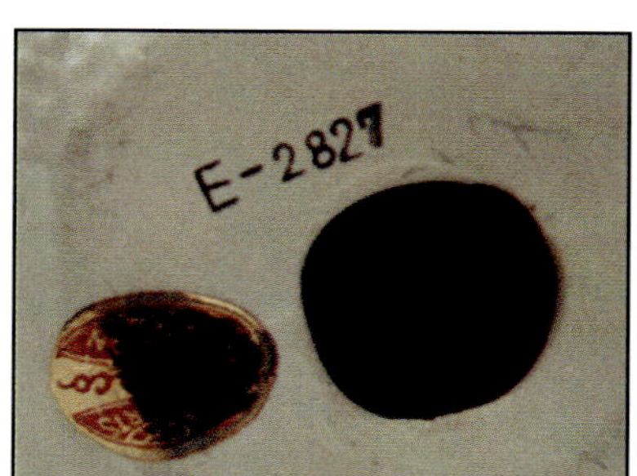

Bottom markings of birthday angel

November Angel, 3.25", E-2827, $18-20

Top left: March-Narcissus Angel, 4", blue and silver label, $18-20

Center left: April-Sweetpea Angel, 4", blue and silver label, $18-20

Bottom left: May-Lily of the Valley Angel, 4", blue and silver label, $18-20

Below: August-Poppy Angel, 4", no mark, $18-20

March Angel, 4.5", red and gold Enesco Japan label, $15-18

February Angel, 4.5", red and gold Enesco Japan label, $15-18

July Angel, 4.5", red and gold Enesco Japan label, $15-18

May Angel, 4", no markings, $15-18

September Angel, 4", red and gold Enesco Japan label, $15-18

October Angel, 4", no markings, $15-18

June Angel, 4", no markings, $15-18

December Angel, 4", red and gold Enesco Japan label, $15-18

January Basket, 3.5", E-7240, $12-15

July Basket, 3.5", E-7240, $12-15

August Basket, 3.5", E-7240, $12-15

September Basket, 3.5", E-7240, $12-15

October boy Angel, 3.75", red and gold Enesco Japan label, $25-30

Blissful Bossy Cow

A 1965 Enesco catalog shows this line of blue and white ceramic ware and calls it "Blissful Bossy Cow." In addition to the pieces pictured, there is a 2.5" double egg cup. There is not a whole lot of collector interest in this line and prices are very reasonable.

Blissful Bossy Cow Collection

Sugar/Marmalade/Cheese Crock, 2.5", E-5107, $12-15

Creamer, 4.25", E-3801, $12-15

Salt and Pepper Shakers, 3", E-5108, $10-12

Busy Biddy

Featuring a perky "Grandma" type of figure, this series is called the "Busy Biddy," as evidenced by the hang tag found on some pieces. In this line are found salt and pepper shakers, toby-style mugs or head vases, spoon rests or wall plaques, tea bag holders, figurines, and planters. The planters are shown in a 1959 catalog and the spoon rests/wall plaques are pictured in a 1965 Enesco catalog. This series is fairly easy to find and although quite collectible, prices are still reasonable.

Busy Biddy Collection

Salt and Pepper Shakers, 4", red and gold Enesco Japan label, $20-25

Hang tag

Salt and Pepper Shakers, 4", no mark, $20-25

Spoon Rest, 7", hang tag, *Courtesy of Denise Dittner*, $18-20

Salt and Pepper Shakers, 4", no mark, $20-25

Spoon Rest, 7", no mark, *Courtesy of Denise Dittner*, $18-20

Spoon Rest, 7", red and gold Enesco Japan label, *Courtesy of Denise Dittner*, $18-20

Hang tag

Spoon Rest, 6", E-4814, $18-20

Tea Bag Holder, 3.5", no mark, *Courtesy of Denise Dittner*, $22-25

Spoon Rest, 7", red and gold Enesco Japan label, $18-20

Spoon Rest, 6", E-4814, $18-20

Planter, 7", 9048, not marked Enesco, $20-25

Figurine, 5.5", no mark, $15-18

Figurine, 5.5", no mark, $15-18

Vase/Toby Mug, 5", C-9062, $25-30

Vase/Toby Mug, 5", C-9062, $25-30

Planter, right facing, 6", C-9065, $20-25

Planter, right facing, 6", C-9065, *Courtesy of Betty Swedien*, $20-25

Planter, left facing, 6", C-9065, *Courtesy of Betty Swedien*, $20-25

Colonial Americana/Kitchen Independence

Often called Kitchen Independence, the original boxes indicate that this line was actually named Colonial Americana, although the egg timer has a marking on the bottom which reads "Kitchen Independence." A rather large line, the salt and pepper shakers, napkin holder, scouring pad/soap holder, and spoon storage are easily found. The Betsy Ross pincushion/tape measure is scarce, but the hardest-to-find piece is a match holder, which just recently surfaced on the Internet and is not shown here. The Betsy Ross cookie jar is difficult to find in good condition—most have major paint loss on the flag portion of the jar. A mint condition cookie jar will sell in the $100 range. Imported in the 1960s but still popular with collectors today.

Salt and Pepper Shakers, 4.25", E-6290, $12-15

Napkin Holder, 5.75", red and gold Enesco Japan label, $15-18

Toothpick Holder, 4.25", E-6293, $15-18

Box showing "Colonial Americana" name

Scouring Pad/Soap Holder, 5.75", red and gold Enesco Japan label, $18-20

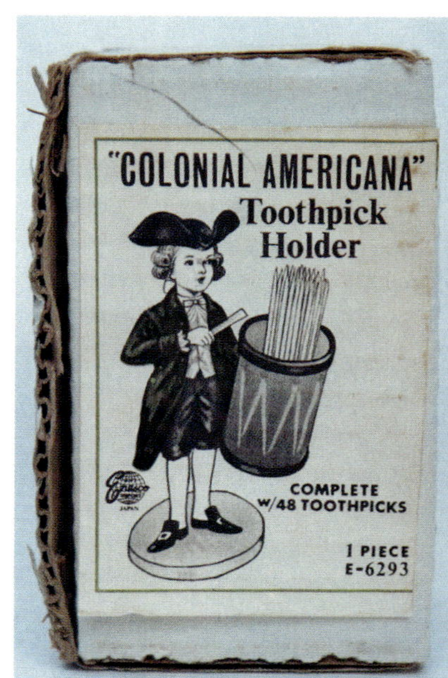

Toothpick Holder box

Egg Timer, 5.5", red and gold
Enesco Japan label, $30-35

Betsy Ross Pincushion/Tape Measure, 4.75",
no mark, $55-60

Pincushion showing tape measure extended

Betsy Ross Spoon Storage, 5.75", red
and gold Enesco Japan label, $20-22

Colonial Americana/Kitchen Independence Collection

Dearie is Weary

"Dearie is Weary" is a very collectible line, much desired by collectors, thus making prices quite high. The sprinkler bottle recently sold for over $800 on the Internet, but this price was not sustained in subsequent auctions. Additional pieces include salt and pepper shakers, a soap dish or scouring pad holder, napkin holder, tumbler, spoon storage stand, tooth brush holder, and tile trivets/plaques. This line is shown in a 1965 Enesco catalog with the following description: To see her - is to pity her - is to love her. "Dearie" will be embraced as the alter ego of every housewife.

Tile Trivet/Plaque, 5.5", E-5285, $12-15

Salt and Pepper Shakers, 4.75", E-5208, $30-35; Scouring Pad/Soap Holder, 5.5", E-5207, $30-35, *Courtesy of Mary O'Malley, Photographer: Carol Schaedig*

Spoon Holder, 6.25", E-5210, *Courtesy of Denise Dittner*, $35-40

Napkin/Recipe Card Holder, 6", E-5209, *Courtesy of Denise Dittner*, $35-40

Tile Trivet/Plaque, 5.5", E-5285, $12-15

Dutch Treat

Often called "Dutch Kids," the official name for this line is "Dutch Treat." It is a rather large line and quite popular. It consists of salt and pepper shakers, creamer and sugar, teapot, toothpick holder, oil lamp, egg timer, covered dish, wall plaque, ashtray, mugs, and other dinnerware pieces. The salt and pepper shakers are easily found, as are the creamer and sugar and teapot. Not as plentiful are the oil lamp, egg timer, covered dish, ashtray, mugs, and dinnerware pieces. All items are found with the red and gold Enesco Japan label and probably date from the 1960s.

Dutch Treat Collection

Teapot, 6", E-5822, $30-35

Salt and Pepper Shakers, 2.5", E-5816, $10-12

Toothpick Holder, 3.25", E-6803, $20-25

Marking on Toothpick Holder

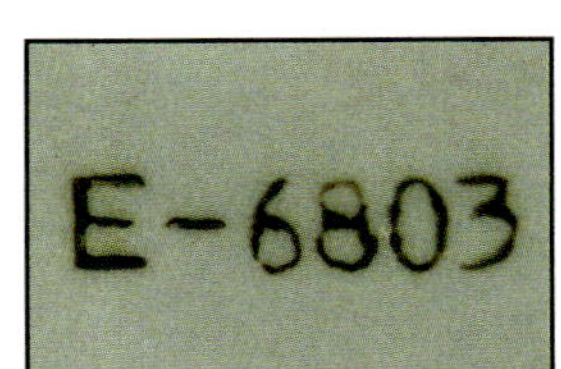

Sugar and Creamer, 4" and 3.5", E-5817, $25-30

Wall Plaque, 10.25", E-5821, $20-25

Box showing "Dutch Treat" name

Egg Timer, 4.5", E-6101, $45-50

Oil Lamp, shade is missing, 8", E-5823, $25-28, with shade $32-35

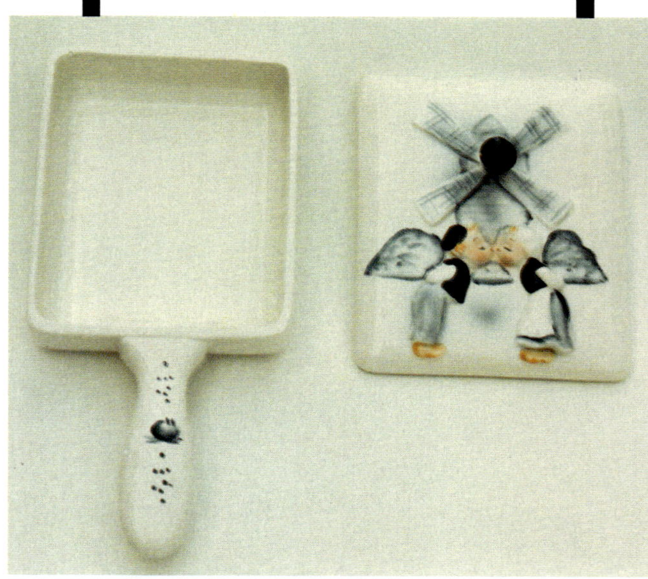

Covered Dish, 8" long, E-5820, $35-40

Festive Poinsettia

Most of the importing companies featured a line of accessories with a Christmas theme. Enesco's Christmas set was called "Festive Poinsettia" and was dark green with red poinsettia trim. There are quite a few pieces in this line that show up from time to time on the Internet. The red and gold label indicates that this line probably dates from the 1960s. All items shown are from the collection of Betty Swedien.

Salt and Pepper Shakers, 3.5", red and gold Enesco Japan label, *Courtesy of Betty Swedien*, $8-10

Candleholders, 3", red and gold Enesco Japan label, *Courtesy of Betty Swedien*, $10-15

Creamer and Sugar, 4" and 5.25", red and gold Enesco Japan label, *Courtesy of Betty Swedien*, $15-18

Candy Dish, 6.5", Enesco stamped in black on bottom, *Courtesy of Betty Swedien*, $10-12

Pitcher, 7.25", black Enesco print on bottom, *Courtesy of Betty Swedien*, $20-22

Divided Dish, 9.75", "Festive Poinsettia" label, *Courtesy of Betty Swedien*, $20-22

Napkin Holder, 5", red and gold Enesco Japan label, *Courtesy of Betty Swedien*, $10-12

Mugs, 4.25", no mark, *Courtesy of Betty Swedien*, $2-3 each

Covered Dish, 6.5", red and gold Enesco Japan label, *Courtesy of Betty Swedien*, $22-25

Cookie Jar, 9.5", no mark, *Courtesy of Betty Swedien*, $20-22

Figurines

Most importing companies of the 1950s and 1960s featured a large line of figurines, and Enesco was no exception. Many different types of figurines were popular collectibles and had broad market appeal. All figurines shown are from the 1950-1960 time period.

3 Piece Dog Set, 5.25" and 2.5", no mark, $10-15

"Papa" Dog, 5", red and gold Enesco Japan label, $8-10

The "Lovin' Lions" Figurines, 3.75", blue and silver label, $10-12

Pair of Figurines, 7.25", E-2085, $22-25

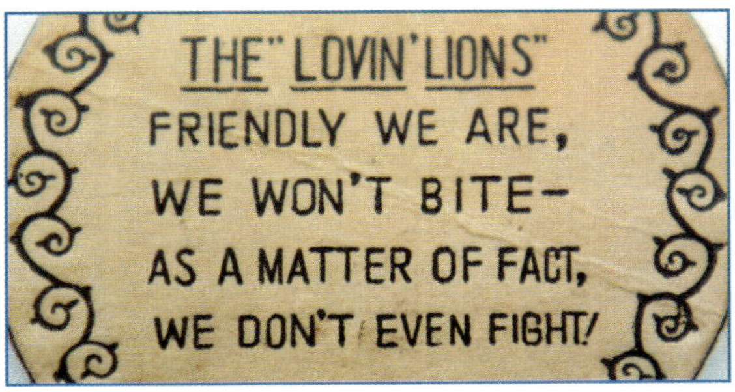

"Lovin' Lions" hang tag

"Roslyn" the Red Imp, 5.5", E-4265, $12-15

"Roslyn" the Red Imp, 5.25", E-4265, $12-15

Christmas Figurine, 5", blue and silver label, $10-12

"Roslyn" the Red Imp, 3", E-4265, $12-15

"The Perfume Imp," (shown in 1965 catalog with perfume atomizer), 4.25", E-4804, $8-10

Teen Age Figurine, 4.75", C-8072, $10-12

Middle Age Sportsman Figurine, 6", blue and silver label, $10-12

Figurines, 4", blue and silver label, $12-15

Teen Age Figurine, 5", C-8072, $10-12

Middle Age Sportsman Figurine, 6", blue and silver label, $10-12

Happy Painter, 4", blue and silver label, $8-10

His Royal Highness the Prize Winner, 4.5", red and gold Enesco Japan label, $10-12

Golden Girls

This is a very large line, and very collectible. The Golden Girls are young ladies in bonnets and long dresses, ornamented with rhinestones. The line came in three colors: brown, pink, and yellow. Brown is the color most often found, followed by yellow and then pink. Many different pieces are in this line and there are two types of bonnets worn by the girls, one with a wide brim and one with a narrow brim. In addition, some pieces can be found with a hat shaped like flower petals, although these are scarcer. Prices are still reasonable on most pieces. The salt and pepper shakers are easily found, while the lipstick holders, cotton ball holders, bobby pin holders, and trinket boxes are harder to find. This line is usually found with the red and gold Enesco Japan label, which dates it to the early 1960s. In addition, there is a label usually attached to the side of the item which states that it is called "Golden Girls" by Enesco.

Golden Girls Collection

Salt and Pepper Shakers, 3.5", red and gold Enesco Japan label, $15-20

Condiment Jars, 3.5", red and gold Enesco Japan label, $25-28 pair

Trinket Box, 5.5", red and gold Enesco Japan label, *Courtesy of Denise Dittner*, $35-40

Condiment Jars on Double Tray, 3.5", Tray 6.25" long, no mark, $35-40 set

Planter, 5.25", no mark, $25-30

Salt and Pepper Shakers and Bell on Triple Tray, Bell 4", Tray 9.5" long, red and gold Enesco Japan label, *Courtesy of Denise Dittner*, $45-50

Planter, rose petal hat, 5.25", red and gold Enesco Japan label, $30-35

Head Vase, small brim hat, 3.25", no mark, *Courtesy of Denise Dittner*, $35-40

Lipstick Holder, 5.5", red and gold Enesco Japan label, *Courtesy of Denise Dittner*, $35-40

Bobby Pin Holder, 3.5", *Courtesy of Denise Dittner*, $35-40

Cotton Ball Holder, Rose Petal Hat, 5.5", E-2075, *Courtesy of Denise Dittner*, $30-35

Head Vase, large brim hat, 3.5", no mark, $35-40

Salt and Pepper Shakers, 3.5", red and gold Enesco Japan label, $15-20

Head Vases showing both hat styles, 3.25", no mark, *Courtesy of Worthington-Johnson Family*, $35-40 each

Condiment Jars on Double Tray, 3.25", Tray 6.25" long, red and gold Enesco Japan label, $35-40

Salt and Pepper Shakers and Bell on Triple Tray, Bell 4", Tray 9.5" long, red and gold Enesco Japan label, *Courtesy of Denise Dittner*, $45-50

Lipstick Holder, 5.5", E-2074, $35-40

Head Vase, small brim hat, 3.25", $35-40 ($.69 original price)

Cotton Ball Holder, rose petal hat, 5.5", E-2075, $30-35

Trinket Box and Male Figurine, Box 5.5", Figurine 5", E-2075 (box), *Courtesy of Denise Dittner*, Box $35-40, Figurine $15-18

Golden Girls Label

Salt and Pepper Shakers and Bell on Triple Tray, red and gold Enesco Japan label, $45-50

Golden Girls Collection

Salt and Pepper Shakers, 3.5", no mark, $15-20

Cotton Ball Holder, rose petal hat, 5.5", E-2075, $30-35

Bell, 4", Golden Girls label, $15-20

Lipstick Holder, 5.25", E-2074, *Courtesy of Denise Dittner*, $35-40

Bobby Pin Holder, rose petal hat, 3.5", E-2071, $40-45

Head Vase, small brim hat, 3.25", Golden Girls label, $35-40

Golden Girls Collection

Planter, 5", Golden Girls label, $25-30

Lipstick Holder Collection

Head Vases

Head vases are very popular with collectors and prices remain high, although stabilized. Some Enesco head vases sell for high prices because they are in shorter supply than those of other companies. The "High Teens," "Smart Teens," "Bouquet and Mink," "Sophisticated Teens," and "Smart Girls" are especially popular with collectors and command high prices. A set of three Walt Disney head vases called "Fairy Tales Come True" and consisting of Alice in Wonderland, Cinderella, and Snow White are very hard to find and the most expensive of the Enesco head vases. Most of the Enesco vases were manufactured in the 1950-1960 time period.

Delsey Tissue Girls Head Vases, 5.5", no mark, *Courtesy of Worthington-Johnson Family*, $85-110 each

"Teen Age" Head Vases, 5.75", E-7013, *Courtesy of Worthington-Johnson Family*, $110-135 each

"Velvet Bow" Head Vase, 5.75", E-4029, *Courtesy of Worthington-Johnson Family*, $110-135

"Teen-Rific" Head Vases, 5.75", 5.25", E-8028, *Courtesy of Worthington-Johnson Family*, Left $125-150, Right $225-250

"Babushka Girl" Head Vase, 5.75", E-5025, *Courtesy of Worthington-Johnson Family*, $125-150

"Necklace Girl" Head Vase, 5.25", E-6054, *Courtesy of Worthington-Johnson Family*, $110-135

"Hat Girl" Head Vase, 5.5", E-6055, *Courtesy of Worthington-Johnson Family*, $135-150

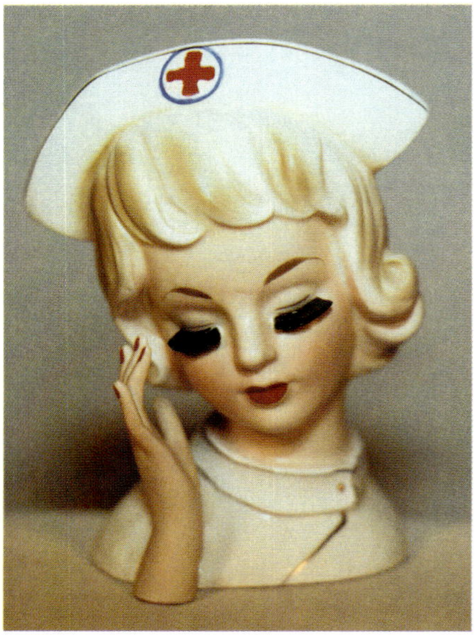

"Favorite Nurse" Head Vase, Rare, 5.5", E-4032, *Courtesy of Worthington-Johnson Family*, $350-400

Girl with Kitten Head Vase, 5.5", no mark, *Courtesy of Worthington-Johnson Family*, $75-85

"Teen-Rific" Head Vase, 6", E-8029, *Courtesy of Worthington-Johnson Family*, $110-135

Girl With Telephone Head Vase, 4.75", E-8482, *Courtesy of Worthington-Johnson Family*, $75-85

Right: "Cutie Pie" Head Vase, 5", E-4095, *Courtesy of Worthington-Johnson Family*, $65-80

Center left: "Sophisticated Teens" Head Vases, Left 5.5", E-0296, Center 5.75", E-0297, Right 5.5", E-0296, *Courtesy of Worthington-Johnson Family*, Left $135-165, Center $150-165, Right $185-225

Bottom left: "Teen Age" Head Vases, 5.75", 4", E-8027, *Courtesy of Worthington-Johnson Family*, $95-125, $85-110

"Teen Age" Head Vases, 5", E-8027, *Courtesy of Worthington-Johnson Family*, $85-110

"Demure Ladies with Earrings" Head Vases, 4.5", E-6053, *Courtesy of Worthington-Johnson Family*, Left $110-135, Right $85-110

"Demure" Lady Head Vases, 4.5", E-6053, *Courtesy of Worthington-Johnson Family*, Left $110-135, Right $85-110

"Demure" Head Vase, Rare, 4.5", E-5027, *Courtesy of Worthington-Johnson Family*, $225

"Sophisticated Lady" Head Vase, 7", E-4095, *Courtesy of Worthington-Johnson Family*, $225-265

Head Vases, 5.5", 6.25", no mark, *Courtesy of Worthington-Johnson Family*, $110-125, $250-300

Teen Age Head Vase, 7.25", no mark, *Courtesy of Worthington-Johnson Family*, $275-325

"Mother" Head Vase, Part of Mother and Daughter Set, 6.25", E-4090, *Courtesy of Worthington-Johnson Family*, $110-135

"Girl with Hand" Head Vase, 7.25", E-6057, *Courtesy of Worthington-Johnson Family*, $235-285

"Smart Girl" Head Vase, Rare, one of three known head vases with sunglasses, 7.25", E-9013, *Courtesy of Worthington-Johnson Family*, $1200-1500

"Smart Girl" Head Vase, 7", E-9013, *Courtesy of Worthington-Johnson Family*, $300-350

"Girl with Hands" Head Vase, 7", E-6057, *Courtesy of Worthington-Johnson Family*, $250-285

"Smart Girl" Head Vase, 7.25", E-9013, *Courtesy of Worthington-Johnson Family*, $300-350

"Girl with Hands" Head Vase, 7", E-6057, *Courtesy of Worthington-Johnson Family*, $250-285

"Smart Girl" Head Vase, 7", E-9013, *Courtesy of Worthington-Johnson Family*, $300-350

"Girl with Hands" Head Vase Collection

"Smart Girl" Head Vase Collection

"Bouquet and Mink" Head Vases and Planter Collection

"Bouquet and Mink" Head Vase/Wall Pocket, 6", C-8996, $80-85

"Bouquet and Mink" Head Vase/Wall Pocket, 6", C-8996, $80-85

"Southern Belle" Bud Vase/Place Card Holder, 3.25", C-8062, *Courtesy of Denise Dittner*, $40-45

Girl with Kitten Head Vase, 5.75", red and gold label, *Courtesy of Denise Dittner*, $75-85

Head Vase, 5", E-1190, $25-30

Head Vase, 5", E-1190, $25-30

"Blanket Baby" Head Vase, 5.5", E-4091, $40-45

Helpful Kitchen Pixie

Pixies are always popular collectibles and most importing companies had a line of pixie items. Enesco's Helpful Kitchen Pixies consisted of salt and pepper shakers, an egg timer, toothpick holder, and air freshener. All can be found fairly easily and prices are reasonable.

Salt and Pepper Shakers, 4", E-5217, $12-15

Box for Salt and Pepper Shaker set

Scouring Pad/Soap Holder, 6", red and gold Enesco Japan label, $12-15

Egg Timer and Recipe Holder, 5.5", red and gold Enesco Japan label, $35-40

Air Freshener, 3", E-5218, $15-18

Air Freshener box

Hang tag from Air Freshener

Hopper the Frog

For want of a better name, we will call this line "Hopper the Frog," although that may not be the official Enesco title. The frog line closely resembles the Beaver Dam and Swifty Turtle series and all three lines were probably in production at the same time. This line is very collectible, as are the beaver and turtle pieces, and prices are fairly high. Found with the red and gold Enesco Japan label, probably early 1960s.

Jam Jar, 4.5", red and gold Enesco Japan label, $25-30

Salt and Pepper Shakers, 3.25", red and gold Enesco Japan label, $18-20

Jelly Jar, 4.5", red and gold Enesco Japan label, $25-30

Sugar and Creamer, 3.5", red and gold Enesco Japan label, $30-35

Humpty Dumpty

This is one of the nicest of the older Enesco lines; expect to pay high prices for the rarer pieces. Shown in the 1958 Enesco catalog, it was called "Mr. and Mrs. Humpty-Dumpty" Kitchen and Pantry Ware. Each piece originally had a descriptive, poetic string tag which read as follows:

Humpty-Dumpty Had a Cute Wife
She was in the Kitchen Most of Her Life

Most of the Humpty Dumpty pieces no longer have their blue and silver Enesco label and therefore are not usually recognized as having been an Enesco product. The taller set of salt and pepper shakers, although made exactly like the smaller Enesco shaker set, is actually a Lipper and Mann import. During that time period, pieces were not copyrighted and any company could copy another company's product. There is also a square planter with the same Humpty Dumpty figure on it but it bears a Napco label and is hard to find. The salt and pepper shakers are the most plentiful; the cookie jar, grease jar, and oil and vinegar cruets are more rare and quite expensive if in good condition. The cookie jar, teapot, wall pockets, and spoon rests were made in two styles: Mr. Humpty-Dumpty and Mrs. Humpty-Dumpty.

Salt and Pepper Shakers, small size, 4.5", C-8352, black Japan imprint, $18-20

Sugar and Creamer Set, 4.5", C-8351, *Courtesy of Jean Payne*, $40-45

Salt and Pepper Shakers, large size, 6", Lipper and Mann label, *Courtesy of Jean Payne*, $18-20

Teapot - Mr. Humpty, 8.5", C-8350, *Courtesy of Jean Payne*, $75-80

Wall Pocket/Planter - Mrs. Humpty, 7.5", C-8357, *Courtesy of Jean Payne*, $45-50

Wall Pocket/Planter - Mr. Humpty, 7.5", C-8357, *Courtesy of Jean Payne*, $45-50

Grease Jar (part of Range Set), 5", C-8353, *Courtesy of Jean Payne*, $55-60

Spoon Rest - Mrs. Humpty, 6.75", C-8355, $45-50

Spoon Rest - Mr. Humpty, 6.75", C-8355, $45-50

Mr. and Mrs. Humpty Dumpty Collection

Kitchen Pixie

A delightful set, shown in a 1958 Enesco catalog on the same page as the Humpty-Dumpty line. This is another set which is usually missing its label and normally not credited as being an Enesco product. The catalog states that a cleverly worded string tag was attached to each item, but this tag was not found on any of the pieces shown here. Nothing in this line is easily found, and there is usually some red paint loss on the pieces that do surface. In addition to those items shown here there is a cookie jar and a grease jar. Prices can go quite high, depending on condition and availability.

Teapot, 6.5", C-8122, $90-95

Salt and Pepper Shakers, 3.5", C-8120, $35-40

Wall Pocket/Planter, 5.5", C-8121, $75-80

Sugar and Creamer, 4.5", C-8123, $50-55

Lady Planters

As companion pieces to the lady head vases, the full length lady planters are popular collectibles. Value varies depending on size and amount of detail. Dates of manufacture of the planters shown were in the 1950s and 1960s.

"Bouquet and Mink" Planter, right facing, 8", E-7294, *Courtesy of Diane Thompson*, $50-55

"Flower Basket" Planter, 7", E-4088, $20-22

"Flower Basket" Planter, 7", E-4088, *Courtesy of Diane Thompson*, $20-22

"Bouquet and Mink" Planter, left facing, 8", E-7294, $50-55

"Flower Basket" Planter, 7", E-4088, $20-22

Girl Planter, 6.75", no mark, $20-22

"Portrait Girl" Planter, 6.5", E-6114, $18-20

Girl Planter, 6.5", E-3146, $20-22

"Girl on Tree Swing" Planter, 5.5", E-5070, $20-22

"Portrait Girl" Planter, 6.5", E-6114, $18-20

Teen Age Girl Bud Vase, 5.75", E-4258, $20-22

"Bonnet Belle" Planter, 5.5", E-5022, *Courtesy of Diane Thompson*, $20-22

"Springtime Girl" Planter, 6", E-7011, *Courtesy of Diane Thompson*, $20-22

Double Planter, rare, 7", red and gold Enesco Japan label, *Courtesy of Diane Thompson*, $50-55

Planter, 8", E-2077, *Courtesy of Diane Thompson*, $20-22

"Pony-Tail" Girl Planter, 6", E-5057, $18-20

Planter, 8", red and gold Enesco Japan label, *Courtesy of Diane Thompson*, $25-28

"Flower Sheath" Planter, 6.5", label, *Courtesy of Mary O'Malley, Photographer: Carol Schaedig*, $25-28

Planter, 7", red and gold Enesco Japan label, *Courtesy of Diane Thompson*, $20-22

"The Pony Tail Girl" Planter, 6", C-8064, *Courtesy of Diane Thompson*, $18-20

Planter, 5", red and gold Enesco Japan label, $15-18

"Labelle" Planter, 8.25", E-7294, $30-35

"Rosebud Girl" Planter, 6.25", C-9080, *Courtesy of Diane Thompson*, $18-20

Planter, 5.25", red and gold Enesco Japan label, *Courtesy of Denise Dittner*, $15-18

Miscellaneous

In this section are miscellaneous pieces, too few to have their own category.

Mary Poppins Medicine Spoon Holder, 5.5", WDE-122, $45-50

Lipstick Holder, 5.5", red and gold Enesco Japan label, $20-22

Toothpick Holder, 2.25", red and gold Enesco Japan label, $8-10

Toothpick Holder, 2.25", red and gold Enesco Japan label, $8-10

Toothpick Holder/Vase, 5.75", E-3840, *Courtesy of Denise Dittner*, $15-18

Bobby Pin Holder, 4.25", red and gold Enesco Japan label, *Courtesy of Betty Swedien*, $15-18

Wall Plaque, 7", E-9808, $15-18

Rural Life Kids Book Ends, 5.25", blue and silver label, C-8081, $30-35

Gramp's False Teeth Holder, 3.5", C-8340, $10-12

Juice Set, 7.75" and 3.5", red and gold label, black Japan stamped on bottom, $18-20

Gram's False Teeth Holder, 3.5", C-8340, $10-12

Oil Lamp, 10", red and gold Enesco Japan label, $18-20

Lord's Prayer Wall Plaque/Planter, 8.25", E-4314, $10-12

"For Old Time's Sake" Smoking Figurines, 6", E-9972, $18-20

"Young Lady" Night Light with Perfume Pocket, 6", E-9308, $18-20

Smoking Figurines box

Wall Plaque, left facing, 7", E-8981, $12-15

"Tea for Two" Musical Teapot, 6", E-5833, *Courtesy of Denise Dittner*, $30-35

Wall Plaque, right facing, 7", E-8981, $12-15

Angel Fish Wall Crest Set, 6" and 3.5", C-8108, *Courtesy of Mary O'Malley, Photographer: Carol Schaedig*, $18-20

Gay Nineties Bottle Stopper, 3.5", C-8193, $6-8

Gay Nineties Bottle Stopper, 3.5", C-8193, $6-8

Gay Nineties Bottle Stopper, 3.5", C-8193, $6-8

"Climbing Siamese Cat" Wall Piece, 8" long, E-5129, *Courtesy of Mary O'Malley, Photographer: Carol Schaedig*, $12-15

The Gay Nineties Bottle Stopper Set in box

Gay Nineties Bottle Stopper, 3.5", C-8193, $6-8

Teen Ager Wall Plaque, 11", red and gold Enesco Japan label, $25-30

Swan Console Set, 5.25" and 2.75", E-4244, $18-20

Swan Candleholders, 2.75", E-4244, $8-10

Sailor Napkin Rings, 3.5", E-1283, $20-25

Sailor Napkin Rings box

Teen Ager Wall Plaque, 11", red and gold Enesco Japan label, $25-30

Bon Bon Nut Dish, 4.5", blue and silver label, C-8237, $10-12 pair

Missy Mouse

Not many pieces are found in this line, but those that are seem to be quite collectible. A silver label attached to each piece identifies it as "Missy Mouse."

Salt and Pepper Shakers, 2.25", E-1164, $12-15

Toothpick Holder, 2.25", E-1163, $12-15

Missy Mouse label

Condiment Jar, 4", E-1167, $18-20

Mother Goose's Children

A collection of six nursery rhyme characters, each with an identifying string tag, shown in a 1958 Enesco catalog. Not easily found, it is possible to find a complete set with much searching. The set consists of Little Miss Muffet, Little Bo Peep, Little Boy Blue, Little Jack Horner, Little Red Riding Hood, and Old King Cole.

Little Red Riding Hood Figurine, 6.25", blue and silver label, C-8046, $15-18

Little Boy Blue hang tag

Little Boy Blue Figurine, 6", blue and silver label, C-8046, $15-18

Mother-in-the-Kitchen

The "mother" of them all, Mother-in-the-Kitchen is the most popular and widely collected of the older Enesco lines. First introduced in the 1950s, these older pieces are found with labels other than Enesco, indicating they were probably imported by different companies under Enesco's direction. A 1965 Enesco catalog shows a fairly large display of Mother-in-the-Kitchen pieces, but only in the pink color. These pieces are found with the red and gold Enesco Japan label. Often called "Prayer Lady," the official Enesco name is "Mother-in-the-Kitchen." Prices vary according to the rarity of the piece, with the blue color prices slightly higher and white pieces trimmed in blue commanding the highest prices. There is no problem finding Mother-in-the-Kitchen pieces on the Internet, but expect to pay more for the hard-to-find items. In the pink color, the salt and pepper shakers, napkin holder, and toothpick holder are very plentiful and are the most reasonably priced items in the line.

Salt and Pepper Shakers, 4.5", E-3348, $10-15

Toothpick Holder, 4.25", E-5199, $15-20

Napkin Holder, 6.25", E-2826, $15-20

Candleholders, rare, 4", *Courtesy of Betty Swedien*, $375-400

Spoon Storage, 6.25", E-4811, $35-40

Bank, 5.75", red and gold label, *Courtesy of Betty Swedien*, $115-125

Sugar and Creamer, 4", red and gold label, *Courtesy of Betty Swedien*, $140-150

Scouring Pad/Soap Holder, 5.75", E-4246, $30-35

Teapot, 6", red and gold label, *Courtesy of Betty Swedien*, $125-135

Bell, 4.5", E-2825, *Courtesy of Betty Swedien*, $75-85

Spoon Rest, 5.75", E-3347, *Courtesy of Betty Swedien*, $40-45

Air Freshener, 5", E-5200, *Courtesy of Betty Swedien*, $120-130

Wall Plaque, 7.5", E-3349, $35-40

Instant Coffee Jar, 6", red and gold label, *Courtesy of Betty Swedien*, $100-110

Bud Vase, 6", E-5197, *Courtesy of Betty Swedien*, $185-195

Egg Timer/Telephone Timer, 5.75", E-4810, *Courtesy of Betty Swedien*, $65-70

Planter, 6.25", E-3824, *Courtesy of Betty Swedien*, $110-115

Stringholder, 6", no mark, *Courtesy of Betty Swedien*, $200-225

Ring Holder, 5.75", E-4247, *Courtesy of Betty Swedien*, $90-100

Crumb Brush and Pan, 8.5", no mark, *Courtesy of Betty Swedien*, $200-215

Napkin Holder, 6.25", stamped Enesco, E-8122, $25-30

Picture Frame, 6", E-4809, *Courtesy of Betty Swedien*, $300-325

Salt and Pepper Shakers, 4.5", E-3348, *Courtesy of Betty Swedien*, $38-40

Napkin Holder box

Cookie Jar, 10", no mark, *Courtesy of Betty Swedien*, $245-255

Scouring Pad/Soap Holder, 5.75", E-4246, *Courtesy of Betty Swedien*, $40-45

Toothpick Holder, 4.25", red and gold Enesco Japan label, $30-35

Mug, 4", no mark, *Courtesy of Betty Swedien*, $100-115

Napkin Holder, 6.5", red and gold label, *Courtesy of Betty Swedien*, $50-55

Salt and Pepper Shakers, 2.75", red and gold label, *Courtesy of Betty Swedien*, $40-45

Coffee Jar, 6", red and gold Enesco Japan label, $150-155

Toothpick Holder, 4.25", no mark, *Courtesy of Betty Swedien*, $35-40

Toothpick Holder, 4.25", red and gold Enesco Japan label, $12-15

Mother-in-the-Kitchen Variations

The popularity of the Mother-in-the-Kitchen line prompted other companies to import their own version of this very collectible series. Even Enesco had variations of the prayer lady pieces. In Canada, a set was distributed using the Giftcraft label, showing a girl in a yellow checked dress with white apron and white dust cap, her hands folded in prayer. The captions on the pieces were written in French, and the set may be seen in Chapter Four. In a 1978 Norcrest catalog, this same set—called Praying Gingham Girl—is shown with English writing. It also came in a deep green and a raspberry color but these colors are seldom found.

Salt and Pepper Shakers, 4", red and gold Enesco Japan label, $12-15

Toothpick Holder, 4.25", no mark, *Courtesy of Denise Dittner*, $15-18

Salt and Pepper Shakers, 4.5", red and gold Enesco Japan label, $15-18

Napkin Holder, 6.25", red and gold Enesco Japan label, $18-20

Napkin Holder, color variation, red and gold Enesco Japan label, $18-20

Cookie Jar, 9", Giftcraft Toronto label, Shown in Norcrest 1978 catalog as Praying Gingham Girl Tableware, $40-45 (see same set with French captions in Chapter Four)

Mother's Little Helper

An appealing line, called "Mother's Little Helper" according to the label found on many of the pieces. Not a very well known series; a piece shows up from time to time but not often enough to be considered easy to find.

Salt and Pepper Shakers, 3.75", red and gold label, *Courtesy of Denise Dittner*, $20-25

Toothpick Holder, 3.75", red and gold label, *Courtesy of Denise Dittner*, $12-15

Figurine, 4", Mother's Little Helper label, *Courtesy of Denise Dittner*, $10-12

Napkin Holder, 5.5", red and gold label, *Courtesy of Denise Dittner*, $12-15

Figurine, 4", Mother's Little Helper label, *Courtesy of Denise Dittner*, $10-12

Scouring Pad/Soap Holder, 5.25", red and gold label, *Courtesy of Denise Dittner*, $12-15

Mouse and Cheese

Showing up often, this line is quite collectible and prices are very reasonable.

Scouring Pad/Soap Holder, 3.5", red and gold Enesco Japan label, $10-12

Salt and Pepper Shakers, Mouse 3.5", Cheese 1.25", red and gold Enesco Japan label, $10-12

Covered Dish, 5.5", red and gold Enesco Japan label, $12-15

Toothpick Holder, 3.5", red and gold Enesco Japan label, $12-15

Napkin Holder, 4", black stamp "Japan," $12-15

Planters

Always popular, planters were a large part of every importing company's product line. They were made in all styles and for every occasion. Enesco was one of the few companies that did not import a large line of holiday planters and figurines. Very few Christmas and Valentine items are found bearing the Enesco label.

Taurus Planter, one of set of twelve zodiac planters with zodiac fortune tag, 5", E-0335, $25-30

Angel Fish Planter, 6.5", red and gold Enesco Japan label, $12-15

The Little Old Lady Who Lived In A Shoe Planter, left facing, 7.75", C-8048, $30-35

Youngsters and Old Folks Planter, 5.5", blue and silver label, C-8047, $18-20

"Angel in the Clouds" Planter, 4", red and gold Enesco Japan label, E-7012, $20-22

Youngsters and Old Folks Planter, 5.5", blue and silver label, C-8047, $18-20

"Just Boys" Planter, 6.5", E-5062, $12-15

Polka Dot Skirt and Legs

A very delightful set consisting of salt and pepper shakers, napkin holder, and toothpick holder. There were three different color combinations: green polka dots with blue shoes, pink polka dots with yellow shoes, and yellow polka dots with brown shoes.

Salt and Pepper Shakers, 3.5", red and gold Enesco Japan label, $12-15

Salt and Pepper Shakers, 3.5", red and gold Enesco Japan label, $12-15

Toothpick Holder, 3.25", no mark, $12-15

Napkin Holder, 4", no mark, $12-15

Polka Dot Skirt Collection

Sad Hound

An appealing hound dog with a tear rolling down his cheek is the subject of this series. There are quite a few different pieces in this line, most of them easily found and reasonably priced.

Spoon Rest, 6.5", red and gold Enesco Japan label, $10-12 ($.89 original cost)

Salt and Pepper Shakers, 4", red and gold Enesco Japan label, $10-12

Scouring Pad/Soap Holder, 5", red and gold Enesco Japan label, $10-12

Ketchup Container, 4.75", red and gold Enesco Japan label, $10-12

Mustard Container, 4.75", red and gold Enesco Japan label, $10-12

Bank, 6.5", red and gold Enesco Japan label, $15-18

Salt and Pepper Shakers

Always popular with collectors, salt and pepper shakers were a staple of every importing company. Every possible subject was depicted, limited only to the designer's imagination.

Pink Cow Salt and Pepper Shakers, 2.75", blue and silver label, $12-15

Clubs Salt and Pepper Shakers, one of a set of four, 2.25", 4.25" with stand, blue and silver label, $18-20

Cat Salt and Pepper Shakers, 3" and 2", blue and silver label, C-8217, $10-12

Bear Salt and Pepper Shakers, 3.5", red and gold Enesco Japan label, $12-15

Poodles with Rhinestones Salt and Pepper Shakers, 4.25", red and gold Enesco Japan label, $18-20

Owl Salt and Pepper Shakers, 3.25", E-6108, $12-15

Men Salt and Pepper Shakers, 3.25", *Courtesy of Mary O'Malley, Photographer: Carol Schaedig*, $18-20

Grandma and Grandpa Salt and Pepper Shakers, 4.75", *Courtesy of Denise Dittner*, $10-12

Prunella & Pomeroy Pig, Styled by Lorraine Elam, 3.5", red and gold Enesco Japan label, $18-20

Dr. Owl Salt and Pepper Shakers, 3.75", red and gold Enesco Japan label, $20-22

The Daisy Babies Salt and Pepper Shakers, 2.5", blue and silver label, C-8085, $15-18

"Soulful Clown" Salt and Pepper Shakers, 3.5", E-6093, $18-20

Comical Salt and Pepper Shakers, 4.75", red and gold label, *Courtesy of Denise Dittner*, $15-18

Black Cats Salt and Pepper Shakers, 5.75", blue and silver label, $20-25

Siamese Cats

Cat figurines are always popular. Enesco's Siamese cat had a jeweled collar around its neck and is quite appealing to collectors judging by how quickly these pieces sell on the Internet.

Siamese Cat Lipstick Holder, side view, 6.5", E-3342, $18-20

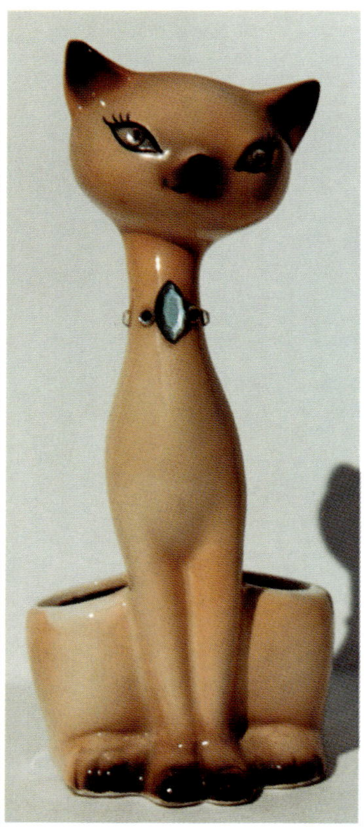

Siamese Cat Lipstick Holder, front view, 6.5", E-3342, $18-20

Siamese Cat Bobby Pin Holder with magnet, 6.5", red and gold Enesco Japan label, $18-20

Siamese Cat Figurine, 6.25", red and gold label, *Courtesy of Kim Lambert*, $25-28

Siamese Cat Figurine, 6.25", red and gold label, *Courtesy of Kim Lambert*, $25-28

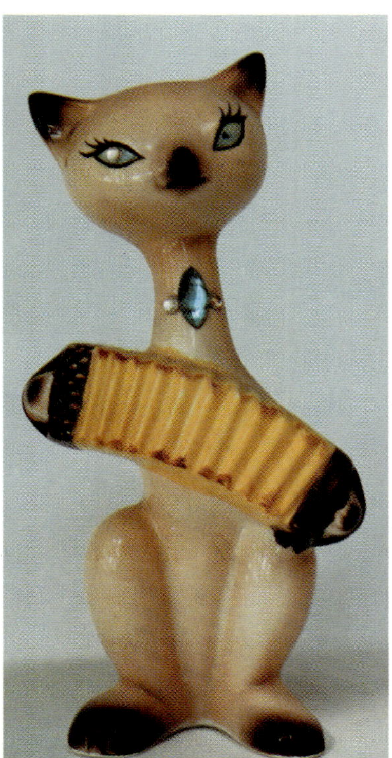

Siamese Cat Figurine, 6.25", red and gold label, *Courtesy of Kim Lambert*, $25-28

Snappy the Snail

A rather large line, and very popular with collectors. Some pieces are fairly easy to find, a few are rare and show up very seldom. The plastic antennae are quite often missing or broken; items in mint condition are hard to come by. Pieces in this set are salt and pepper shakers, creamer and sugar, teapot, bank, ashtray, spoon rest, planter/wall pocket, tea bag holder, lollypop/candy jar, and cookie jar. A 1959 catalog shows this line.

Salt and Pepper Shakers, 3.75", red and gold Enesco Japan label, $20-25

Sugar and Creamer, 5", red and gold Enesco Japan label, $30-35

Bank, 4.5", red and gold Enesco Japan label, $30-35

Snappy Snail Collection

"Lollypops-Candy Jar," rare, 7.5", red and gold Enesco Japan label, $75-80

Sweet Shoppe

Considering that this was a rather large line, the pieces are not that easy to find. One of the problems is that when put up for sale on the Internet, it is very seldom called "Sweet Shoppe." The various pieces were furnished with a string tag that read "Sweet Shoppe" and if the tag is missing it is usually not identified. The line consisted of a savings bank with padlock and keys (two different, pink and blue), a girl dinner bell, a candy or lollypop jar that came in both pink and blue, girl/boy figurines, girl/boy salt and pepper shakers, girl/boy double planter, and cookie jar.

Salt and Pepper Shakers, 3.5", C-8041, $18-20

Shaker, 3.5", C-8041, $8-10

Double Planter, 6.75", C-8044, $20-25

Salt and Pepper Shakers, 3.5", blue and silver label, C-8041, $18-20

Sweet Shoppe hang tag

Bell, 4.5", C-8043, $15-18

Candy or Lollypop Jar, 6", blue and silver label, C-8331, $20-22

Candy or Lollypop Jar, 6", C-8331, $20-22

Swifty the Turtle

Complementing the beaver and frog line, Swifty the Turtle is shown in a 1958 Enesco catalog. Items in the line include a cookie jar, savings bank with padlock, ashtray/standing ornament, spoon rest, and salt and pepper shakers. Not in plentiful supply, it takes some searching to find a complete set.

Salt and Pepper Shakers, 3.5", red and gold Enesco Japan label, $18-20

Spoon Rest, 6.5", no mark, $18-20

Ashtray or Standing Ornament, 8", C-8333, $18-20

Winkin' Kitten

A very popular line, Winkin' Kitten was imported in the same time frame as the Mother-in-the-Kitchen series. A salt and pepper set has been found with a Calaco label. Most of the other pieces bear the red and gold Enesco Japan label. The harder-to-find pieces are the tape measure and the cookie jar. The square planter came in both pink and blue and is the most rare piece, seldom seen.

Salt and Pepper Shakers, 3", Calaco Imports label, $15-18

Teapot, 5", no mark, $40-45

Toothpick Holder, 2.5", E-8460, *Courtesy of Kim Lambert*, $12-15

Salt and Pepper Shakers, color variation, 3", $15-18

Sugar and Creamer, 3.5" and 4", no mark, *Courtesy of Kim Lambert*, $25-30

Toothpick Holder box

Condiment Jar, 4", label, *Courtesy of Kim Lambert,* $18-20

Planter, rare, 5.25", no mark, *Courtesy of Kim Lambert*, $55-60

Pin Cushion/Tape Measure, rare, 3", red and gold Enesco Japan label, $60-65

Coffee Jar, 4.5", *Courtesy of Kim Lambert*, $25-30

Calaco Imports label found on some Winkin' Kitten pieces

Shown with tape measure extended

Winkin' Kitten Collection

Woodland Friends

A miniature animal assortment, consisting of twelve different styles, squirrels, bunnies, raccoons, beavers, chipmunks and woodchucks. They are fur trimmed, matte finished in semi-porcelain, and are shown in a 1965 Enesco catalog.

Raccoon Figurines, 3", E-0169, $8-10 each

Squirrel Figurines, 3", E-0169, $8-10 each

Squirrel Figurines, 3", E-0169, $8-10 each

Beaver Figurines, 3", E-0169, $8-10 each

Squirrel and Bunny Figurines, 3", E-0169, $8-10 each

Raccoon and Bunny Figurines, 3", E-0169, $8-10 each

Bunny Figurine, 3", E-0169, $8-10

Woodland Friends Collection

Chapter Two
1970s and 1980s

Animals

Animal novelty items comprised a large part of the inventory of all the importing companies, Enesco included. Cute little animals dressed in finery and doing "people" things appealed to a large segment of the population and sold extremely well.

Cat and Mouse Figurine, 3.75", gold and black Taiwan label, $12-15

"Puppy -Toes" Figurine, 5", gold and black Taiwan label, $15-18

"Puppy -Toes" Figurine, 2.25", gold and black Taiwan label, $10-12

"Puppy -Toes" Figurine, 3", gold and black Taiwan label, $10-12

Markings on bottom of Puppy-Toes Figurines

Country Calico Mice Figurine, 3.75", red and gold Taiwan label, $12-15

Bear Figurine, 2.5", gold and black Taiwan label, $10-12

Bear Figurine, 2.5", gold and black Taiwan label, $10-12

Bear Figurine, 3", gold and black Taiwan label, $10-12

Bone China Set, 2.5", red and gold Japan label, $10-12

Bone China Set, 2.75", red and gold Japan label, $10-12

Bear Figurine, 3", gold and black Taiwan label, $10-12

Dog Figurine, 2.5", red and gold label, $8-10

Pig Figurine, 4", no mark, $10-12

Dog Figurines, 2.5" and 3", red and gold label, $8-10 each

Pig Figurine, 2.75", gold and black Taiwan label, $8-10

Pig Figurine, 4", no mark, $8-10

Pig Figurine, 4.25", no mark, $8-10

Pig Figurine, 2.5", gold and black Taiwan label, $8-10

Pig Figurine, 2.5", gold and black Taiwan label, $8-10

Rabbit Figurine, 5", black stamp Enesco 1979, $12-15

Pig Figurine, 2", gold and black Taiwan label, $8-10

Annette Little Exercising Frogs, 3.75" long, red and gold Enesco Japan label, $6-8 each

Anthropomorphic Fruit

Anthropomorphic fruit people appeal to a broad category of collectors. Enesco's anthropomorphic line is not easy to find and there is a lot of competition for the harder-to-find pieces. The toothpick and napkin holders are easiest to find, other pieces to the set show up only occasionally.

Napkin Holder, 4.25", E-0302, $15-18

Toothpick Holder, 2.5", E-0301, $10-12

Scouring Pad/Soap Holder, 3.5", no mark, $15-18

Napkin Holder, 4.25", E-0302, $15-18

Spoon Rest (Napkin Holder and Toothpick in background), 5.5", no mark, *Courtesy of Mary O'Malley, Photographer: Carol Schaedig*, $15-18

Toothpick Holder, 2.5", E-0301, $10-12

Napkin Holder, 4.25", E-0302, $15-18

Toothpick Holder, 2.5", E-0301, $10-12

Toothpick Holder, 2.5", E-0301, $10-12

Creamer, 3.5", E-0309, $15-18

Shaker Sets on stand, rare, 9.5", E-0305, $50-55

Set of Napkin Holders

Birthday Sets

Birthday sets continued to be popular in the 1970s and 1980s. The Growing Up Girl line was the most extensive and most popular of Enesco's birthday imports. First introduced in 1982, Growing up Girls continued to sell well in the 1990s.

July Girl, 3.5", no mark, $8-10

August Girl, 3.5", butterfly label Enesco Taiwan, $8-10

September Girl, 2.25", red and gold Enesco Japan label, $10-12

March Angel, 3.75", red and gold Enesco Japan label, $10-12

Tenth Birthday Girl on Music Box, plays "Happy Birthday," 4.5", no mark, $15-18

April Angel, 3.75", red and gold Enesco Japan label, $10-12

Twelfth Birthday Girl with hang tag, 3", Taiwan label, $10-12

Wednesday's Child, 4", E-4712, $12-15

Second Birthday Girl, 3", Taiwan label, $10-12

Markings on bottom of Wednesday's Child

Sunday's Child, 4", E-4712, $12-15

For a Boy Who's 1 Figurine, 4.25", red and gold Enesco Japan label, $10-12

For a Boy Who's 3 Figurine, 5", red and gold Enesco Japan label, $10-12

For a Boy Who's 4 Figurine, 5", red and gold Enesco Japan label, $10-12

January Girl, 3.75", Enesco/Malaysia, $10-12

Growing Up Birthday Girls hang tag

Photo Frame, Two Year Old, 4.5", gold and black Korea label, $10-12

Growing Up
Two Year Old
Birthday Girl, 3",
E-9526, $8-10

Growing Up Birthday Sport Girls and Boys hang tag

Growing Up Three Year
Old Birthday Sport Girl,
3.5", E-4103, $10-12

Growing Up Five Year
Old Birthday Sport Girl,
4", E-4105, $10-12

Growing Up Three Year Old
Birthday Girl, 3", Enesco
Korea label, $8-10

Growing Up Five Year
Old Birthday Girl, 3.75",
Enesco Korea label,
$10-12

Growing Up Four Year
Old Birthday Sport Girl,
3.5", E-4104, $10-12

Growing Up Fifth Christmas Birthday Girl, 4", E-5225, $10-12

"My Fifth Christmas" bottom imprint

Growing Up Sixth Christmas Birthday Girl, 4", Taiwan label, $10-12

Growing Up Boys, Three Year Old Christmas, 3.75", $10-12

Growing Up Boys, Four Year Old Christmas, 4", $12-15

Hang tag, Growing Up Boys - Christmas

Growing Up Boys, Two Year Old Christmas, 3.75", $10-12

Country Calico Mice, Days of the Week, Thursday, 3.75", red and gold Taiwan label, $12-15

Country Calico Mice, Days of the Week, Friday, 3.75", red and gold Taiwan label, $12-15

Country Cousins

These endearing figurines are actually patterned after real-life country cousins by artist Ellen Williams, who is Aunt Ellen to the cousins. The cousins are called Katie, Scooter, Skip, Sarah, and Polly. From time to time other family members make an appearance. There are over 750 Country Cousin figurines and they have remained popular from their time of inception in the early 1980s. The more intricate sets, which comprise several different pieces, are the most sought after and command the highest prices. The single figurines are not as much in demand and sell at a more reasonable price, but all of the Country Cousin line is very collectible.

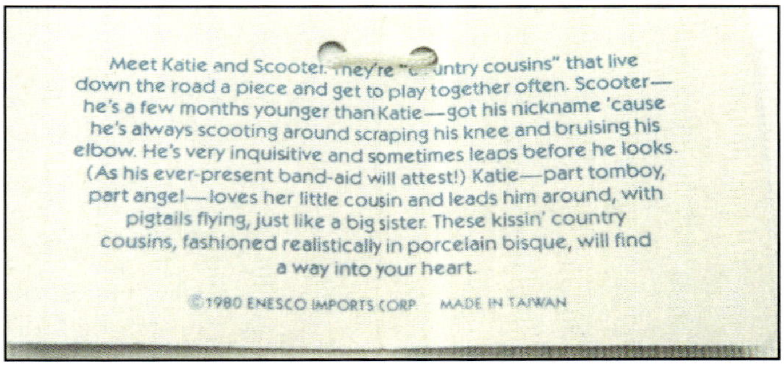

Country Cousins hang tag

Country Calico Mice, Days of the Week, Saturday, 3.75", red and gold Taiwan label, $12-15

Country Cousins box

Bottom markings, Country Calico Mice, Days of the Week

Scooter on Tractor, 5", dated 1985, *Courtesy of Nancy Huppert*, $40-45

Scooter and Katie, 2.75" and 3.25", dated 1981, *Courtesy of Nancy Huppert*, $10-15 each

Katie, 3.5", dated 1985 and 1980, *Courtesy of Nancy Huppert*, $8-10 each

Katie on Snowmobile, 4", dated 1984, *Courtesy of Nancy Huppert*, $25-35

Katie, 3.5" and 3.75", dated 1982 and 1985, *Courtesy of Nancy Huppert*, With Pig $8-10, With Sheep $10-15

Scooter pulling Skip on Sled, 3.5", dated 1985, *Courtesy of Nancy Huppert*, $20-25

Sarah, Polly and Skip, 6", dated 1981, *Courtesy of Nancy Huppert*, $25-30

Scooter, 3.25" and 4", dated 1983 and 1984, *Courtesy of Nancy Huppert*, With Grill $20-25, With Mower $15-18

Scooter and Skip, 5" and 2.75", dated 1984 and 1986, *Courtesy of Nancy Huppert*, Ringmaster $10-15, With Pinwheel $8-10

Skip, Scooter and Katie, 4.75" and 2.5", dated 1981 and 1984, *Courtesy of Nancy Huppert*, With Bunnies $6-8, Leap Frog $12-15

Katie, 3" and 4", dated 1980 and 1991, *Courtesy of Nancy Huppert*, Caroling $8-10, With Present $6-8

Katie and Scooter, 3.75" and 3.5", dated 1983 and 1985, *Courtesy of Nancy Huppert*, $12-15 each

Scooter and Katie, 3.5", dated 1982 and 1988, *Courtesy of Nancy Huppert*, With Flowers $8-10, With Valentines, $6-8

Scooter, Skip and Katie, 4" and 3.25", dated 1990, *Courtesy of Nancy Huppert*, On Sled $20-22, Snowball $10-12

Sarah and Polly, 3.25", dated 1986, *Courtesy of Nancy Huppert*, $10-12

Katie and Scooter, 5", gold and black label, *Courtesy of Nancy Huppert*, $20-25

Scooter and Katie, 3.25" and 4", *Courtesy of Nancy Huppert*, $10-15 each

Katie and Scooter, 4.5", dated 1981, *Courtesy of Nancy Huppert*, $20-25

Katie and Scooter, 3", 3.75", 5", dated 1981 and 1983, *Courtesy of Nancy Huppert*, Nativity Music Box $60-65, Figurines, $8-10

Sarah and Skip, 4.75", dated 1985, *Courtesy of Nancy Huppert*, $20-25

Scooter and Katie, 5.5", gold and black label, *Courtesy of Nancy Huppert*, $22-25

Sarah, Polly and Katie, 3", dated 1984, *Courtesy of Nancy Huppert*, $10-15 each

Polly and Skip, 4", dated 1985, *Courtesy of Nancy Huppert*, $20-25

Sarah and Scooter, 4", dated 1984, *Courtesy of Nancy Huppert*, $15-20

Sarah, 2.75" and 4", dated 1983 and 1985, *Courtesy of Nancy Huppert*, Sitting $6-8 each, Standing $8-10

Katie and Scooter, 4", dated 1983, *Courtesy of Nancy Huppert*, $20-25 each

Scooter, 3.25", dated 1981 and 1985, *Courtesy of Nancy Huppert*, $8-10 each

Aunt Betty and Skip, 4", dated 1985, *Courtesy of Nancy Huppert*, $20-25

Sarah, 3.25", dated 1987, $8-10

Skip, 2.75", dated 1987, $8-10

Skip Fishing, 3.5", dated 1985, $15-18

Scooter, 3.5", dated 1985, $20-25

Katie, 4.25", dated 1982, $12-15

Polly as Gymnast, 2" and 2.5", E-3541, $6-8 each

Polly as Gymnast, 2.25" and 2.75", E-3541, $6-8 each

Bottom marking on Polly as Gymnast

County Fair

A collection of porcelain bisque figurines from 1983, designed by Christina Mae Risley.

County Fair Collection hang tag

"Courtney," 4.5", E-4151, $12-15

"Helene," 4.5", E-4151, *Courtesy of Denise Dittner*, $12-15

"Jennie," 4.5", E-4151, *Courtesy of Denise Dittner*, $12-15

Dear God Kids

A large and popular line, first introduced in the early 1980s by artist Anne Fitzgerald. Very collectible and still selling well on the Internet.

Figurine, 5", gold and black Enesco Korea label, *Courtesy of Denise Dittner*, $12-15

Figurine, 3.25", gold and black Enesco Korea label, $12-15

Figurine, 3.25", gold and black Enesco Korea label, $12-15

Figurine, 4.75", black and gold Enesco Korea label, *Courtesy of Denise Dittner*, $12-15

Figurine, 4.75", black and gold Enesco Korea label, *Courtesy of Denise Dittner*, $12-15

Delbies

According to the Delbies' hang tag, a Delbie is a "pink-cheeked, wide-eyed, devilishly innocent-looking cutie with a smile that radiates from ear to ear." After that description, who could resist adding a Delbie to their collection? They were created by artist Del McLaughlin in 1982 under the Del Graphics name.

Delbies tag, outside view

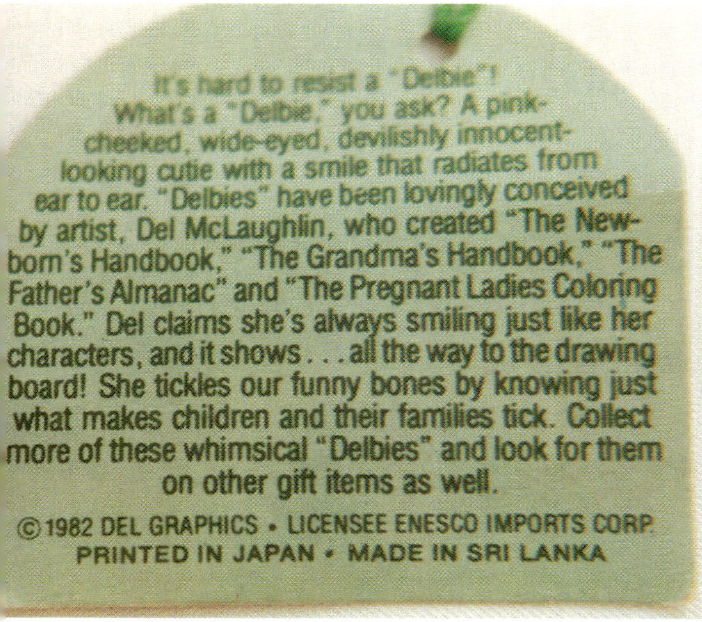

Delbies tag, inside view

Figurine, 4.25", Del Graphics label on bottom, $8-10

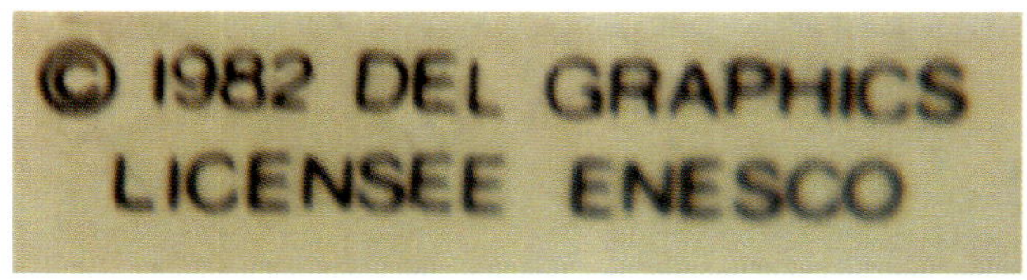

Del Graphics label

Figurine, 4.25", Del Graphics label on bottom, $8-10

Figurine, 4.25", Del Graphics label on bottom, $8-10

Figurines

All importing companies relied on figurines to make up a large part of their business. The ones shown here are not hard to find and are reasonably priced.

First Communion Girl Figurine, 6", black stamp Enesco Japan, $12-15

Eggbert "Eggsucator" Figurine, 3.25", #764582, $12-15

Choir Boy Bell, 3.75", red and gold butterfly label, Taiwan, $10-12

Choir Boy Bell, back view, 3.75", red and gold butterfly label, Taiwan, $10-12

Eggbert "Eggsercizer" Figurine, 3.25", #764531, $12-15

Glass Fruits with Fairy, 1.75", #393657, $3-4 each

Glass Fruits with Fairy, 1.75", #393657, $3-4 each

Maruri Masterpiece Bone China Figurine, 3.5", red and gold Enesco Taiwan label, $12-15

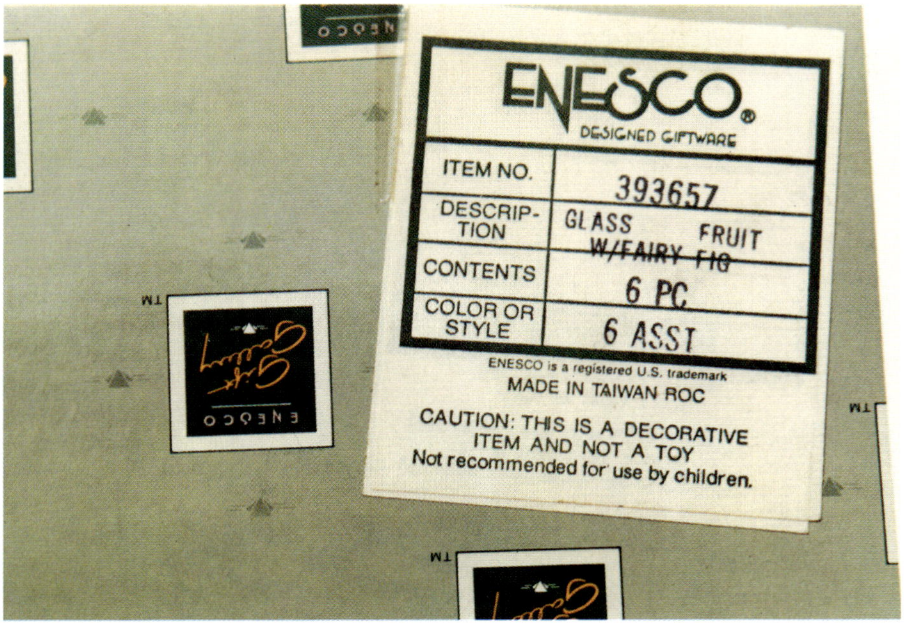

Glass Fruit box

Garfield Candle, 2.25", $10-12

Lorlipop Dragon Trast Figurine, 4", gold and black Enesco Taiwan label, $10-12

Bottom markings, Lorlipop Dragon Trast

Garfield Figurine, 4.25", black and gold Enesco Korea label, 1978-1981 United Feature Syndicate, $15-18

Garfield

Who doesn't love that rascally character Garfield? Enesco's Garfield was first introduced in 1978 and continues to be a favorite collectible.

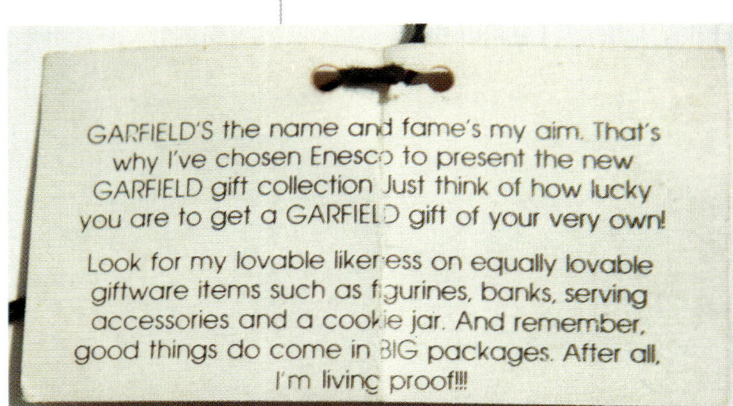

Hang tag, Garfield Figurine

Garfield Figurine, 4.5", black and gold Enesco Korea label, $12-15

Garfield Figurine, 2.75", black and gold Enesco Korea label, $12-15

Treasury of Christmas Ornament, 3.25", #558695, $10-12

Garfield Figurine, 4.5", black and gold Enesco Korea label, $12-15

Garfield Figurine, 2.75", hang tag, $12-15

Treasury of Christmas Ornament, "Fast Track Cat," 2.25", #585289, $10-12

Garfield Bank, 5", black and gold Enesco Korea label, $18-20

Garfield Figurine, 3.75", black and gold Enesco Korea label, $15-18

Human Beans

Introduced in 1981, Human Beans are loveable characters much prized by collectors. Flaking paint is the biggest problem with Human Beans, but they make up for it with their whimsical charm.

Figurine, 3", gold and black Enesco Sri Lanka label, $15-18

Human Bean hang tag

Marking on Human Bean Figurine

Figurine, 4.25", gold and black Enesco Sri Lanka label, $12-15

Figurine, 4.25", gold and black Enesco Sri Lanka label, $10-12

Figurine, 4.25", 1981 Morgan Inc., $15-18

Christmas Figurine, 4.25", gold and black Enesco Sri Lanka label, $15-18

Figurine, 3.5", gold and black Enesco Sri Lanka label, $15-18

Christmas Ornaments, 3", gold and black Enesco Sri Lanka label, $10-12 each

Mug, 3.5", 1981 Morgan, Inc., $8-10

Kitchenware

During the 1970s and 1980s, Enesco imported many different lines of kitchenware. The animal lines are the most popular, especially the poodle and butterfly line which sells very quickly for rather high prices when pieces of it can be found.

Owl Napkin Holder, 3.75", black Japan stamp, $10-12

Owl Creamer and Sugar, 2.75" and 3.5", red and gold Enesco Japan label, $20-22 set

Rooster Pitcher, 6", red and gold Enesco Japan label, $20-22

Owl Toothpick Holder, 2.25", black Japan stamp, $8-10

Rooster Butter Dish, 3.25", red and gold Enesco Japan label, $20-22

Rooster Napkin Holder, 4", red and gold Enesco Japan label, $15-18

Rooster Pepper Shaker, 6.75", red and gold Enesco Japan label, $8-10

Rooster Salt Shaker, 6.75", red and gold Enesco Japan label, $8-10

Rooster Sugar Bowl, 4.25", red and gold
Enesco Japan label, $12-15

Leaf Design Mugs, 3", red and gold Enesco Japan label, $4-6 each

Rooster Creamer, 3", red and gold
Enesco Japan label, $12-15

Leaf Design Sugar and Creamer, 3.5" and 4.25", red and gold
Enesco Japan label, $12-15

Poodle and Butterfly Salt and Pepper Shakers, 4.5", green
Japan imprint, red and gold label, $18-20

Leaf Design Teapot, 8.25", red and gold Enesco
Japan label, $12-15

Leaf Design Set on Tray

Purple Cat Salt and Pepper Shakers, 2.5", E-1160, $8-10

Purple Cat Spoon Rest/Plaque, 6.25", red and gold Enesco Japan label, $10-12

Purple Cat Scouring Pad Holder, 4", red and gold Enesco Japan label, $10-12

Purple Cat Napkin Holder, 4.25", E-1160, $10-12

Purple Cat Collection with box

"Kettle-Shaped" Salt and Pepper Shakers, 4", red and gold Enesco Japan label, $8-10

"Kettle-Shaped" Relish Jar, 4", E-8345, $8-10

"Kettle-Shaped" Mustard Jar, 4", E-8345, $8-10

"Kettle-Shaped" Condiment Set box

"Kettle-Shaped" Ketchup Jar, 4", E-8345, $8-10

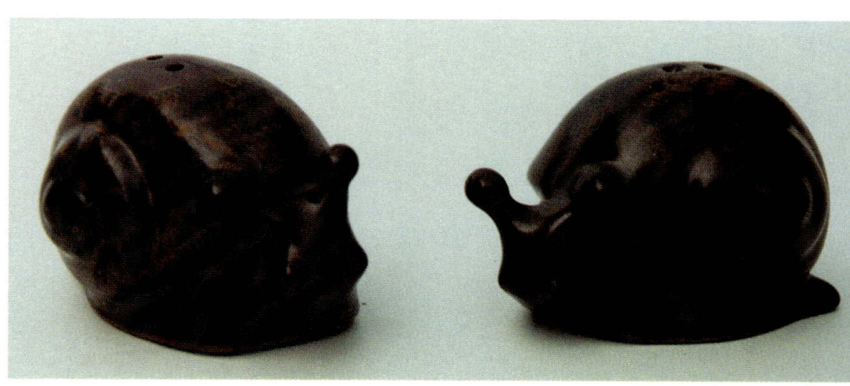

Escargot Salt and Pepper Shakers, 1.75", red and gold Enesco Japan label, $8-10

Escargot Condiment Jar, 4.5", Gourmand Stoneware label, $12-15

Marcia Glynn Canister Set, 7.5", 6", 5", bottom markings, $20-22

Bottom marking on Marcia Glynn pieces

Marcia Glynn Teapot, 5.75", bottom markings, $15-18

Teapot and Mugs, Flower Design, 7.5", 3", Enesco Taiwan label, $12-15 set

Marcia Glynn Sugar and Creamer, 3.5", bottom markings, $15-18

Creamer and Sugar, Flower Design, 4", Enesco Taiwan label, $10-12 set

Salt and Pepper Shakers and Condiment Jar on Tray, 3.25", 4.5", 9" tray, red and gold Enesco Japan label, $15-18

Marking on bottom of Cat Creamer and Sugar

Cat Creamer and Sugar, 3", 3.5", 1982 Enesco stamped on bottom, $18-20

Gentleman Farmer Salt and Pepper Set, 4", 1979 Enesco imprint, $10-12

Gentleman Farmer Creamer and Sugar, 3.5", 1980 Enesco imprint, $18-20

"Gentleman Farmar" marking showing mistake in spelling

Gentleman Farmer Mugs, 3.75", 1980 Enesco imprint, $3-4 each

Gentleman Farmer Teapot, 5.5", 1980 Enesco imprint, $18-20

"Gentleman Farmer" marking showing correct spelling

Marvin

Marvin made his debut in 1983 and was based on a loveable, red-headed comic strip character. Tom Armstrong was the writer and illustrator of Marvin.

Marvin Figurine, 2.5", E-2779C, $8-10

Marvin Figurine, 1.75", E-2779A, $8-10

Marvin Figurine, 2.75", E-2777, $8-10

Marvin Bank, 5.5", gold and black Korea label, $12-15

Marvin Figurine, 3", no mark, $8-10

Marvin Figurine, 2.75", marked Field Enterprises, $8-10

Marvin Comic Strip Figurine, 3", marked 1983, $8-10

Marvin Figurine, 3.25", E-2777, gold and black Korea label, $8-10

Marvin Comic Strip Figurine, 3.25", marked 1983, $8-10

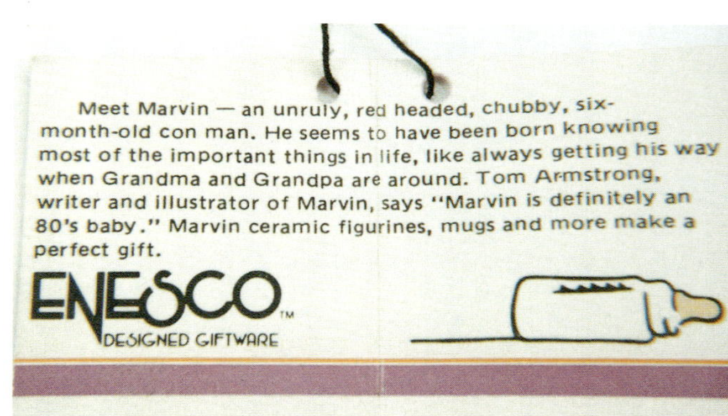

Marvin hang tag

Bottom marking on Marvin Figurines

Marvin hang tag

Marvin Figurine box

Miscellaneous

Shown here are several different types of ceramic imports from the 1970s and 1980s.

Father Mug, 4.5", stamped 1976 Enesco, $10-12

Trinket Box, 4.5", gold and black Enesco Sri Lanka label, $10-12

Mother Mug, 4.5", stamped 1976 Enesco, $10-12

Christmas Bell, 5.25", red and gold Enesco Japan label, $8-10

Thimbles, 1", 1982 Taiwan, $3-4 each

Set of Twelve Thimbles in Case, 8.75", marked Enesco 1982, $25-30

Owl Planter, 4.5", Enesco stamped in black on bottom, $12-15

Marking on back of Thimble Case

Thimbles, 1", 1982 Taiwan, $3-4 each

Turkey Napkin Holder, 3.5", E-9841, $10-12

Suzy's Zoo Bank, 3.25", 1976 by Suzy's Zoo marking on bottom, $10-12

Rodney Rebound Bank, 7.5", 1979 Enesco, $8-10

Here Comes Trouble Cookie Jar, 9", red and gold Enesco Japan label, $30-35

Rodney Rebound sticker

Here Comes Trouble Planter, 5.5", red and gold Enesco Japan label, $15-18

Rabbit Jelly Bean Jar, 8", Kersten Brothers label on bottom, $15-10

Poppyseed Collection

An endearing collection of children figurines known as The Poppyseed Collection. Designed by Barbi Sargent in 1983, the series consists of figurines, music boxes, picture frames, tea sets, and other giftware.

The Poppyseed Collection signage plaque, 4.5", E-3215, $12-15

Poppyseed Figurine, 3.75", E-3202, $12-15

Poppyseed Figurine, 4", E-3205, $12-15

Poppyseed hang tag

Markings on bottom of Poppyseed figurine

Poppyseed Figurine with hang tag, 3.75", E-3201, $12-15

Poppyseed Figurine, 3.5", E-3202, $12-15

Poppyseed Figurine, 3.75", 60372, $15-18

Poppyseed Figurine, 4", E-3205, $15-18

Poppyseed Figurine, 3.75", E-3205, $15-18

Precious Moments

Precious Moments and Enesco are so closely intertwined it is hard to tell them apart. Precious Moments' alliance with Enesco began in 1978 and has continued unabated to the present time, continuing to grow as an important part of Enesco's history. There are so many Enesco Precious Moments products it is impossible to count them all. The items shown here are only a token display of their prolific output—it would take volumes to show them all.

February Figurine, 2.25", 573310, $5-10

May Figurine, 2.25", 573345, $5-10

Precious Moments display

March Figurine, 2.25", 573329, $5-10

January Figurine, 2.25", 573302, $5-10

April Figurine, 2.25", 573337, $5-10

June Figurine, 2.25", 573353, $5-10

July Figurine, 2.25", 573477, $5-10

November Figurine, 2.25", 573892, $5-10

December Figurine, 2.25", 573906, $5-10

August Figurine, 2.25", 573485. $5-10

Lord's Blessing Platter, 15", 254568, $20-25

September Figurine, 2.25", 573493, $5-10

October Figurine, 2.25", 573884, $5-10

Puppy Love Night Light, $8-10

National Day of Prayer Commemorative Figurine, "America You're Beautiful," 4.75", #528862, *Courtesy of Heather Gifford*, $12-15

Nativity Music Box, "Come Let us Adore Him," 6.75", E-2810, *Courtesy of Heather Gifford*, $15-18

Decorating Tree Night Light, 1993, 7.5", *Courtesy of Heather Gifford*, $10-12

Sugar Town Doctor's Office, *Courtesy of Betty Swedien,* $115-120

Night Light Figurine, 1993, 8.25", *Courtesy of Heather Gifford*, $10-12

Sugar Town Train Station, *Courtesy of Betty Swedien*, $115-120

Sugar Town Church, *Courtesy of Betty Swedien*, $90-100

Bell, "Mother Sew Dear," 5.5", E-7181, *Courtesy of Heather Gifford*, $8-10

Figurine, "I Will Always be There for You," 6", #523631, *Courtesy of Heather Gifford*, $15-18

Figurine, "The Purr-fect Grandma," 5.25", #E-3109, *Courtesy of Heather Gifford*, $10-12

Musical, "Let's Keep in Touch," #102520, *Courtesy of Tammy Nash,* $20-25

Figurine, "God's Speed," 4.75", E-3112, *Courtesy of Heather Gifford*, $10-12

Figurine, "The First Noel," 4.5", E-2366, *Courtesy of Heather Gifford*, $8-10

Plaque, "You Have Touched So Many Hearts," 4.5", *Courtesy of Heather Gifford*, $3-4

Sugar Town Skating Rink, *Courtesy of Betty Swedien*, $90-100

Sugar Town School, *Courtesy of Betty Swedien*, $115-120

Chapter Three
1990s

Boys Will Be Boys

Designed by Kim Lawrence, this series of figurines was patterned after her son Blake. A lucky marble is placed somewhere on each piece.

Boys Will Be Boys hang tag

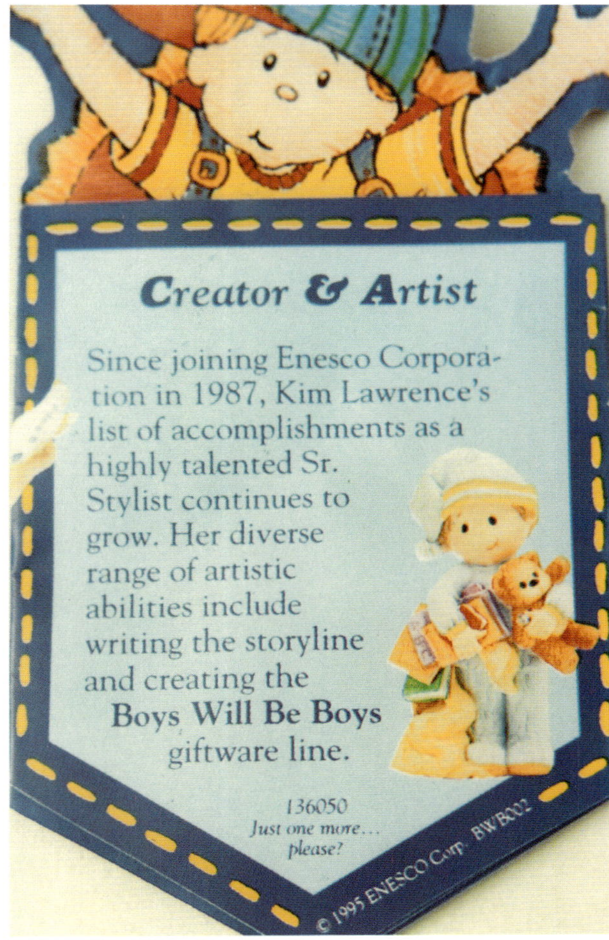

Boys Will Be Boys hang tag

"Teddy was Hungry" Figurine, 3", #136077, $4-5

"Coming in for a Landing" Figurine, 3.5", #136085, $4-5

Boys Will Be Boys box

Catch a Wishing Star

Issued in 1995, Catch A Wishing Star was designed by Karen Hahn.

Catch a Wishing Star display

"Wishing You a Season of Love" Figurine, 3", gold Made in China label, $3-4

"Wishing You a Cozy Hug - A Blanket of Love" Figurine, 2.75", gold Made in China label, $3-4

"Wishing You a Star Shower of Dreams" Figurine, 2.75", gold Made in China label, $3-4

"Wishing You a Love That's Heaven on Earth" Figurine, 2.75", gold made in China label, $3-4

Centimental Bears

Centimental Bears were designed by Peter Fagan in 1995. Peter's extensive antique teddy bear collection was the inspiration behind these endearing reproductions. Each bear has his own name and story (written by Peter's wife Frances), and a special coin accompanies each bear to symbolize love and friendship. The original selling prices ranged from $5.00 for the smaller figurines to $17.50 for the larger ones. On the secondary market there is little demand for them.

Centimental Bears display

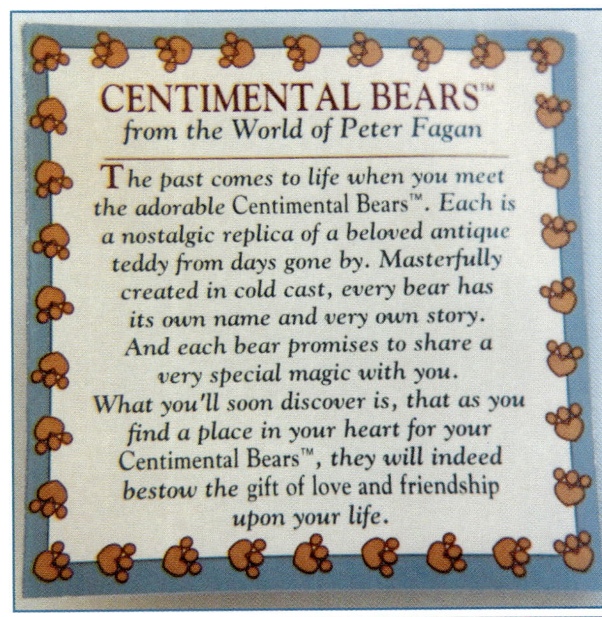

CENTIMENTAL BEARS™
from the World of Peter Fagan

The past comes to life when you meet the adorable Centimental Bears™. Each is a nostalgic replica of a beloved antique teddy from days gone by. Masterfully created in cold cast, every bear has its own name and very own story. And each bear promises to share a very special magic with you. What you'll soon discover is, that as you find a place in your heart for your Centimental Bears™, they will indeed bestow the gift of love and friendship upon your life.

Take This Penny To Heart

Because it's not easy to have your new Centimental Bears™ friend join you on your daily travels, each bear will present you with a special "Centimental" penny. With its tiny heart-shaped silhouette at the center, this "Centimental" penny will serve as a reminder that wherever you go and whatever you do, keep your penny close to your heart and let it fill your days with love and friendship.

Centimental Bears pamphlet

Miranda Figurine, 3", #122424, $2-3

William Figurine, 3", #122386, $2-3

Jack Figurine, 3.25", #122416, $2-3

Centimental Bears box

The Happy Couple Figurine, 2.75", #122440, $2-3

Clarissa and Adrian Figurines, 2.5", #117374 and #125725, $2-3 each

Bernard Figurine, 2.75", #116947, $2-3

Chocolate Chip and Joseph Figurines, 1.25", #116807 and #116823, $1-2 each

Violet and Burt Figurines, 1.5", #125717 and #116823, $1-2 each

Jilly and Morris Figurines, 2", #116548 and #116785, $1-2 each

Teddy Robinson Figurine, 1", #116831, $1-2

Chapeau Noelle

The title of this collection by Lucy Rigg was derived from the French word for hat (wearing hats has become a trademark of Lucy's) and the name of her daughter, Noelle. The bears are sculptured from porcelain bisque and each wears a delightful hat adorned with a feather. Bears in the collection are limited to 5,000 pieces each and are 3.5" tall.

Chapeau Noelle Holiday Display

Holly Figurine, 3.5", #186031, $3-4

Mary Figurine, 3.5", #186031, $3-4

Stephanie Figurine, 3.5", #186031, $3-4

Patty Figurine, 3.5", #186031, $3-4

Chapeau Noëlle™
by Lucy Rigg
Certificate Of Authenticity
Stephanie
Limited to 5,000 Pieces

Lucy Rigg — Noelle Rigg

ENESCO 186031 © 1996 Lucy Rigg & Co. Printed in Taiwan

Chapeau Noelle Certificate of Authenticity

Chapeau Noelle box

Cherished Teddies

One of the most successful of the Enesco collections, Cherished Teddies made their debut in 1992. Based on the illustrations of artist and children's author, Priscilla Hillman, each figurine is sculptured in cold cast resin, given a name, and comes with a certificate of adoption. Because of the popularity and longevity of this series, Cherished Teddies have held their value better than many of the other Enesco lines. All of the figurines shown here are from the collection of Donna Weddle.

Little Bo Peep Figurine, "Looking for a Friend Like You," #624802, $10-12

Cherished Teddies Nursery Rhyme display

Little Jack Horner Figurine, "I'm Plum Happy You're My Friend," #624780, $10-12

Jack and Jill Figurine, "Our Friendship Will Never Tumble," #624772, $15-22

Little Miss Muffet Figurine, "I'm Never Afraid with You at my Side," #624799, $8-10

Mary Mary Quite Contrary Figurine, "Friendship Blooms with Loving Care," #626074, $15-25

Cindy, "This Train is Bound for Holiday Surprises," #219177, $40-45, Kirby, "Heading into the Holidays with Deer Friends," #219118, $30-40, Nick, "Ho, ho, ho, to the Holidays we Go," #219312, $25-35

Casey (Caboose), "Friendship is the Perfect End to the Holiday, #219525, $10-12, Toy Car, "Rolling Along with Friends," #219096, $10-18

Tom Tom the Piper's Son Figurine, "Wherever You Go I'll Follow," #624810, $8-10

Kimberly Figurine, Cherished Seasons Series, "Summer Brings a Season of Warmth," #203335, $10-15

Mail Car - Tony, "A First Class Delivery," #219487, $10-20, Coal Car - Colin, "He Knows If You've Been Bad or Good," #219088, $8-10, Train Engine - Lionel, "All Aboard the Santa Express," #219061, $10-12

Gretchen Figurine, Cherished Seasons Series, "Winter Brings a Season of Joy," #203351, $15-18

Our Cherished Teddies Neighborhood, House, 4.5", #352667, $12-18; Train Station, 4.25", #352683, $12-18

Tasha Figurine, In Grandmother's Attic Series, 1996 Adoption Center Exclusive Event Piece, #156353, $70-90

Lloyd, Railway Conductor, Charter Member Figure, #CT003, $10-15; Kurtis D. Claw Firebear, 1996 Cherished Teddies Club, #CT961, $18-20

Kaitlyn Figurine, Up in the Attic Series, #302600, $30-35

Molly Figurine, "Friendship Softens a Bumpy Ride," #910759, $15-20

Cherished Family display showing Older Son, Older Daughter, Young Son, Young Daughter, and Father, all sell in $5-10 range

Circus Tent display, Bruno (Ringmaster), "Step Right Up and Smile," #103713, $6-10; Seal, "Seal of Friendship," #137596, $5-8; Wally (Clown), "You're The Tops with Me," #103934, $8-10; Circus Tent, #107700, $10-12

Claudia Figurine, "You Take Center Ring with Me," #103721, $8-10

Monthly Friends, Jack (January), "A New Year with Old Friends," # 914754, $10-12; Phoebe (February), "Be Mine," #914762, $6-10; Mark (March), "Friendship is in the Air," #914770, $6-8

Monthly Friends, Alan (April), "Showers of Friendship," #914789, $6-10; May (May), "Friendship is in Bloom," #914797, $6-8; June (June), "Seed of Friendship," #914800, $10-12

Monthly Friends, Arthur (August), "Smooth Sailing," #914827, $6-8; Julie (July), "A Day in the Park," #914819, $15-20; Seth (September), "School Days," #914835, $6-8

Monthly Friends, Oscar (October), "Sweet Treats," #914843, $8-10; Nicole (November), "Thanks for Friends," #914851, $6-8; Denise (December), "Happy Holidays Friend," #914878, $18-20

Michael and Michelle Figurine, "Friendship is a Cozy Feeling," #910775, $35-50

Christopher Figurine, "Old Friends are the Best Friends," #950483, $30-40

Keith and Deborah Figurine, "The Holidays are Twice as Ice," #354244, $15-20

Commemorating 5th Anniversary of Cherished Teddies Production, Featuring Annie, Brittany, Colby, Danny and Ernie, #205354, $12-22

Irish Plaque, #110981, $12-15

We Bear Thanks Series, John, "Bear in Mind, You're Special," #141283, $10-12; Thanksgiving Table, #141542, $10-12; Dina, "Bear in Mind, You're Special," #141275, $8-10

The Birthday Party, 1997 National Event Exclusive, Nina, "Beary Happy Wishes," #215864, $6-10

Patriotic Pals, Sam, "I Want You to be my Friend," #302619, $18-22

Ryan Figurine, "I'm Green with Envy for You," #203041, $15-18

Thanksgiving Prayer Plaque, "We Bear Thanks," #651427, $6-10

Zachary Figurine, "Yesterday's Memories are Today's Treasures," #950491, $15-20

Rainbow Lane Series, Hope, "Our Love is Ever Blooming," #103764, $8-10

Sanford Figurine, "Celebrate Family, Friends and Tradition" #534242, $12-15

Eskimos with Fish Hanging Ornaments, dated 1999 and 2000, #534161, $10-12

Rainbow Lane Series, Jennifer, "Gathering the Blooms of Friendship," #103810, $15-18

Felicia Figurine, "Joy to the World," #533890, $10-12

Bottom right: Bottom markings, Felicia Figurine

Signage plaque, #951005, $6-8

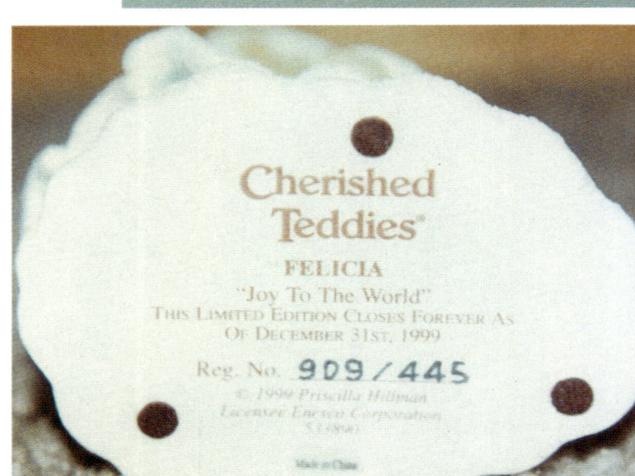

Down Strawberry Lane Display with Tara, Ella, Thelma, Jenna, and Diane

Teddy and Roosevelt Figurine (chair not included with original figurine), "The Book of Teddies," 1993 production only, 90th Anniversary Commemorative Figure, #624918, $45-65

Strawberry Festival Diane and Cherished Seasons Hannah, Diane, "I Picked the Beary Best for You," #202991, $15-20; Hannah, "A Season of Thanksgiving," #203343, $10-12

Alice Figurine, dated 1993 on Muff, "Cozy Warm Wishes Coming Your Way," #912875, $90-100

Priscilla and Greta Figurine, "Our Hearts Belong to You," #128031, $50-65

Priscilla Ann Figurine, 1994 McRand International Collectibles Exposition Exclusive, "There's No One Like Hue," #CRT 025, $100-125

June with Pearl, 4.75", #137375, $30-35

September with Sapphire, 4.75", #137405, $30-35

Coral Kingdom

A very beautiful series, popular with collectors. Fashioned of shimmer stone, crystalline beads that sparkle in the light, Coral Kingdom figurines have appreciated in value.

Coral Kingdom leaflet

December with Turquoise, 4.75", $137448, $30-35

Cute as a Button

Cute as a Button figurines were designed by Mary Rhyner-Nadig. The figurines shown are from the 1993 to 1995 time period.

Button Down Carnival Kid with Popcorn Figurine, 2.5", $3-4

Teacher Figurine, 3.25", #628743, $3-4

Sew Special, "It's a Girl," 2", #167460, $3-4

Button Down Carnival Boy with Mallet Figurine, 4", $3-4

Girl with String of Hearts Figurine, 3.25", #629332, $3-4

Sew Special Birthday, dated 1995, 2.75", $3-4

Boy with Hearts Figurine, 2.75", #629332, $3-4

Circle Embroidery Hoop Photo Frame, 2.75", #629332, $3-4

Disney

The Disney pieces shown here are from the mid 1990s, a small portion of the result of a Disney/Enesco alliance.

Disney Thanksgiving Figurine, 3.5", Made in China, $6-8

Disney Thanksgiving Figurine, 3.25", #220655, $6-8

Mickey and Company box

Mickey Head Vase, 4.75", #292974, $5-7

101 Dalmatians box

Minnie Head Vase, 4.75", #292982, $5-7x

101 Dalmatians Figurine, 2.75", "Lucky I Spotted You for a Friend," #264972, $4-5

101 Dalmatians Figurine, 2.5", "Let's Be Friends," #295167, $4-5

101 Dalmatians Figurine, "Makin' Tracks," #295183, $4-5

101 Dalmatians Figurine, "A Little Bird Told Me...Congratulations," #295175, $4-5

Golf Figurine, 4", #299286, $5-7

Dog Gone Golf

Designed by David Olsen in 1997, these figurines were intended to appeal to the golfing population.

Golf Figurine, 4.5", #299251, $5-7

Golf Figurine, 4.5", #299235, $5-7

Golf Figurine, 4.25", #299243, $5-7

Golf Figurine, 4.25", #299219, $5-7

Golf Picture Frame, 5.5", #299324, $7-10

Down Petticoat Lane

Designed by Patricia Hillman of Cherished Teddies fame, these figurines were produced in 1997, 1998, and 1999.

Stars, Stripes, and Friendship Forever Figurine, 5", #733504, *Courtesy of Denise Dittner*, $8-12

Each Stitch is Sewn with Love and Friendship Figurine, 5", #733490, *Courtesy of Denise Dittner*, $7-10

My Sister, My Very Best Friend Figurine, 4", #318922, *Courtesy of Denise Dittner*, $7-10

I Love Our Heart to Hearts Figurine, 4", #465801, *Courtesy of Denise Dittner*, $7-10

Trinket Box, 4", #541915, *Courtesy of Denise Dittner*, $7-10

Trinket Box, 4", #541893, *Courtesy of Denise Dittner*, $7-10

Shelf Sitter, 4.5", #541850, *Courtesy of Denise Dittner*, $5-7

Li'l Vagabond Figurine, 2.75", no mark, $6-8

Figurines

Figurines are always popular with collectors; the ones shown here all date from the 1990s.

Centaur Figurines, 4", 1994 Thailand, $3-4 each

Li'l Vagabond Figurine, 3.25", Enesco Designed Giftware label, $6-8

Li'l Vagabond Figurine, 3.25", Enesco Designed Giftware label, $6-8

Centaur Figurines, 4", 1994 Thailand, $3-4 each

Jester Figurine, 4", #313963, $4-6

Jester Figurine, 4", #313963, $4-6

Quarterback Football Figurine, 5", #250120, $6-8

Jester Figurine, 3", #313963, $4-6

Running Back Football Figurine, 5", #250120, $6-8

Linebacker Football Figurine, 3", #250120, $6-8

#6 Shooting a Lay Up Figurine, 5", #250155, $6-8

Simpler Days Coca Cola Figurines, 4.5", #639192 and #578738L, *Courtesy of Denise Dittner*, $12-15 each

#3 Figurine, 5.25", #250155, $6-8

Simpler Days Coca Cola Figurine, 4.5", #538914, *Courtesy of Denise Dittner*, $12-15

#22 Shooting Figurine, 5.75", #250155, $6-8

Simpler Days Coca Cola Figurine, 4.75", #578703, *Courtesy of Denise Dittner*, $12.-15

Sesame Street Figurine, Big Bird on Roller Skates, 3", #373729, $10-12

Forever Mother hang tag

Sesame Street Figurine, Bert as Crossing Guard, 4", #373753, $10-12

Forever Mother Perfume Atomizer, 4.25", #305901, $6-8

Forever Mother

Introduced in 1997, Forever Mother is now selling for just a fraction of its original purchase price.

Forever Mother Musical Teapot, plays "Tea for Two," 4", #305812, $10-12

Forever Mother Candleholders, 2", #305928, $8-10 set

Gina's Ballerinas

These pieces were designed by Gina Freehill in 1997 and depict young ballerinas going through the paces.

Gina's Ballerinas Petite Performer Figurine, 4.5", #325740, $8-10

Gina's Ballerinas Practice Makes Perfect Figurine, 6", #325724, $8-10

Gina's Ballerinas Best Foot Forward Figurine, 6", #325716, $8-10

Gina's Ballerinas Tiny Dancer Figurine, 6", #325732, $8-10

Golden League

Designed in 1993 by Don Martin, the Golden League miniature figurines are crafted in cold cast and are Don's interpretation of long ago sports figures.

Golden League Miniatures display

Golden League Figurine, 4.75", #719862, $2-3

Golden League Figurine, 4.75", #719862, $2-3

Golden League Figurine, 4.75", #719862, $2-3

Golden League Figurine, 4.75", #719862, $2-3

Golden League Figurine, 4.75", #719862, $2-3

Growing Up Girls and Growing Up Boys

In 1996, the Afro-American line of Growing Up Girls made its debut. The Christmas Growing Up Boys date from 1994 and the Sports Growing Up Boys are dated 1993.

Growing Up Birthday Girls display

Bottom markings on Growing Up Birthday Girls, 1996

Age 1 Figurine, 2.75", #938556, $2-3

Growing Up Birthday Girls box

Baby Figurine, 3.5" long, #938548, $3-4

Age 2 Figurine, 3", #938564, $3-4

Age 3 Figurine, 3.25", $3-4

Age 4 Figurine, 3.5", #938580, $3-4

Age 5 Figurine, 3.75", #938599, $3-4

Age 6 Figurine, 4", #938602, $4-5

Age 7 Figurine, 4.25", #938610, $4-5

Age 8 Figurine, 4.5", #938629, $4-5

Age 9 Figurine, 4.75", #938637, $4-5

Age 10 Figurine, 5", #938645, $5-6

Age 11 Figurine, 5.25", #938653, $5-6

Age 13 Figurine, 5.75", #938688, $6-7

Age 15 Figurine, 6.75", #938718, $6-7

Age 12 Figurine, 5.5", #938661, $5-6

Age 14 Figurine, 6.25", #938696, $6-7

Age 16 Figurine, 7", #938726, $7-8

Age 16 Musical Figurine, 7", #938777, $15-18

Growing Up Sport Boys hang tag

Age 5 Figurine, 4.25", 1993 Enesco Taiwan, $4-5

Age 7 Figurine, 4.75", 1993 Enesco Taiwan, $4-5

Heavenly Hosts

Heavenly Hosts date from 1996 and were designed by Dennis Brown.

Heavenly Hosts display

Heavenly Hosts hang tag

Inside of Heavenly Hosts hang tag

Postman Figurine, 4", #271934, $2-3

Fireman Figurine, 4.5", #271977, $2-3

Salesman Figurine, 4", #271985, $2-3

Computer Programmer Figurine, 2.75", #272337, $2-3

Doctor Figurine, 4", #271926, $2-3

Baseball Player Figurine, 4.25", #271950, $2-3

Construction Worker Figurine, 4.5", #271942, $2-3

Preacher Figurine, 3.5", #271969, $2-3

School Teacher Figurine, 4.25", #271918, $2-3

Lucy and Me

Designed by Lucy Rigg, this series has been a favorite with collectors since the early 1980s. All figurines shown here were issued in the 1990s.

Hang tag, Lucy & Me

Hang tag, Lucy & Me figurine

Bottom marking on Lucy & Me figurine

Construction Worker, 2.5", #249513, $3-5

Fireman, 3", #229075, $3-5

Doctor, 2.75", $3-5

Nurse, 2.75", $3-5

Postman, 2.75", $3-5

Quilter, 2.5", $3-5

Policeman, 2.75", $3-5

Teacher, 2.75", #249939, $3-5

Chef, 3.25", $3-5

Bobbing for Apples, 2.25", $3-5

Skater, 3.75", $3-5

Road Atlas, 3.5", $3-5

Double Figurine, 2.5", $3-5

On Sled, 2.75", $3-5

Mother and Baby Figurine, 2.25", $3-5

Credit Card, 3", $3-5

Bean Seeds, 3", $3-5

Salsa, 3.5", $3-5

Traveler, 3", $3-5

Tomato Seeds, 3", $3-5

Carrot Seeds, 3", $3-5

Red Hot Chilies, 3", $3-5

In Curlers, 2.75", $3-5

Bath Salts, 3", $3-5

Dentist, 2.5", $3-5

Cosmetic Bag, 2.5", $3-5

Lucy & Me box

Beautician, 3", $3-5

Mary's Moo Moos

One of the most popular of Enesco's collections, Mary's Moo Moos was first introduced in 1993 and designed by Mary Rhyner-Nadig.

Mary's Moo Moos pamphlet

John Deere General Store display

John Deere Figurine, 2", "Farming is Wheel Fun," #674567, $6-8

John Deere Figurine, 2", "A Happy Combine-ation," #674567, $6-8

John Deere Figurine, 2", "A Car Built for Moo," #674567, $6-8

John Deere Collection box

John Deere Figurine, 3", "Udderly Cool," #674516, $8-10

John Deere Figurine, 2.5", "Little Deere, Big Smile," $674559, $6-8

John Deere Figurine, 3", "You're so Deere to Me," #674494, $8-10

Annual LE 1998, 3.75", "Fa-moo-lies Grow with Loving Hearts," #485241, *Courtesy of Kristen Gifford*, $8-10

John Deere Figurine, 2.75", "Stitched with Love from the Heart," #674540, $8-10

5th Annual Commemorative Limited Edition, 1998, 3.75", "Thank Moo for Your Warmth and Friendship," #485268, *Courtesy of Kristen Gifford*, $8-10

Annual LE 1995, 4", "A Moo Addition to our Family," #167576, *Courtesy of Kristen Gifford*, $8-10

Country Wedding Collection, 3.75", "I'll Never Love An-Udder," #138088, *Courtesy of Kristen Gifford*, $6-10

Milkmaid of Honor, 3.5", #167509, *Courtesy of Kristen Gifford*, $6-8

Best Bull, 3.5", #167525, *Courtesy of Kristen Gifford*, $6-8

Wedding Party, 2.75" to 3.5", Flower Girl, Ring Bearer, Milk Maid, Groom Bull, *Courtesy of Kristen Gifford*, $4-8 each

Annual LE 1996, 4", "Watching Over Moo Now and For Heifer," #261858, *Courtesy of Kristen Gifford*, $8-10

Figurine, "Mooey Christmas to Ewe," 2.75", #651656, *Courtesy of Kristen Gifford*, $6-8

Figurine, "Mooey Kissmas," 3.5", #548669, *Courtesy of Kristen Gifford*, $6-8

Annual LE 1997, 3.75", "We Love Our Grandmoo," #319473, *Courtesy of Kristen Gifford*, $8-10

Figurine, "Making a Special Deerlivery," 2.75", #548723, *Courtesy of Kristen Gifford*, $8-10

Figurine, "Shop til the Cows Come Home," 3.25", #651672, *Courtesy of Kristen Gifford*, $6-8

Hoofy New Year Millennium Event Piece 1999, 3.5", #540951, *Courtesy of Kristen Gifford*, $10-12

Figurine, "I Like You and That's Sno Bull," 3.5", #548960, *Courtesy of Kristen Gifford*, $10-12

Figurine, "God's Love is Moo-sic to my Ears," 3.5", #452718, *Courtesy of Kristen Gifford*, $10-15

Figurine, "A Friend is Always There Beside Moo," 3.25", #484873, *Courtesy of Kristen Gifford*, $8-10

Figurine, plays "Silent Night," "Singing Moo Praises," #372439, *Courtesy of Kristen Gifford*, $10-15

Music Boxes, "I'm Dreaming of a White Christmas," 3.25, #274402; "Silent Night, Holy Cow," 3.25", #274410, *Courtesy of Kristen Gifford*, $10-12 each

Ornaments, "Moo-ey Kisses" (Girl), 3.5", #480940; "Me and Moo under the Mistletoe" (Boy), 3.5", #480959, *Courtesy of Kristen Gifford*, $6-8 each

February Birthstone Heart Picture Frame, 3.25", #691410, *Courtesy of Kristen Gifford*, $8-10

Pennant Cows, 2.25", #297933 and #298026, *Courtesy of Kristen Gifford*, $3-4 each

Figurine, "I Love Moo," 2", #468835, *Courtesy of Kristen Gifford*, $4-6

Figurine, "Fishing for Good Wishes," 3", #543241, *Courtesy of Kristen Gifford*, $6-8

Figurine, "May all Moos Dreams Come True," 3.75", #543233, *Courtesy of Kristen Gifford*, $6-8

Figurine, "I'm So Lucky to Know You," 3", #627755, *Courtesy of Kristen Gifford*, $6-8

Figurine, "Cream of the Crop," 2.75", #628859, *Courtesy of Kristen Gifford*, $6-8

Figurine, "Moo are my Little Angel," 2", #372471, *Courtesy of Kristen Gifford*, $6-8

Mini Cows, 2", *Courtesy of Kristen Gifford*, $4-6 each

Figurine, "You are my Sweetie Pie," 3.5", #104272, *Courtesy of Kristen Gifford*, $6-8

Figurine, "I Dig Moo," 3.5", #207098, *Courtesy of Kristen Gifford*, $6-8

Figurine, "Rejoice," 3.75", #468886, *Courtesy of Kristen Gifford*, $8-10

Figurine, "All A-Buzz Over You," 2.75", #159557, *Courtesy of Kristen Gifford*, $6-8

Figurines, 2.5", #207136 (In Flower Pot), #104914 (With Flower Pot), #207136 (Holding Basket), *Courtesy of Kristen Gifford*, $4-6 each

Picture Frame, "Branded with Love," 6", #212741, *Courtesy of Kristen Gifford*, $8-10

Figurines, 2.5", #104914 (all), *Courtesy of Kristen Gifford*, $4-6 each

Figurine, "Merry Christmoos," 3.25", #651702, *Courtesy of Kristen Gifford*, $6-8

Figurine, "Cowgradulations," 4", #296767, *Courtesy of Kristen Gifford*, $8-10

Mini Ornaments, 2.5", Ice Skater 1996, Candy Cane 1994, Bell 1994, *Courtesy of Kristen Gifford*, $4-6 each.

Memories of Yesterday

Designed by Mabel Lucie Attwell, Memories of Yesterday figurines date from the 1990s.

Memories of Yesterday hang tag

Memories of Yesterday dealer's sign

Figurine, "Memories of a Special Day" series, "Thursday's Child has Far to Go," 4.5", #531413, $8-12

Figurine, "Memories of a Special Day" series, "Monday's Child is Fair of Face," 4.5", #531421, $8-12

Figurine, "Memories of a Special Day" series," Saturday's Child Works Hard for a Living," 4.5", #531383, $8-12

Figurine, "Memories of a Special Day" series, "Tuesday's Child is Full of Grace," 4.5", #531448, $8-12

Figurine, "Memories of a Special Day" series, "The Child That is Born on the Sabbath Day," 4.5", #531480, $8-12

Figurine, "Once Upon a Fairy Tale" series, Tweedledum and Tweedledee, 5.5", #526460, $8-10

No Strings Attached signage piece

Tag from Tweedledum and Tweedledee

Figurine, "You Make Being One No Fun," 3.5", #108847, $2-3

No Strings Attached

No Strings Attached is based on a story about a troupe of stringed puppets from the Magical Marionette Theatre. Created and designed by Kim Lawrence, they were issued in 1994.

No Strings Attached display

Trunk Figurine, 1.5", #NSA003, $2-3

Figurine, "Thank You for Supporting Me," 4", #108448, $2-3

Figurine, "You're Always There to Pick Me Up," 2.75", #108995, $2-3

No Strings Attached pamphlet

Figurine, "You Give Me Splinters," 4", #108979, $2-3

Figurine, "You're Really a Softy Inside," 4", #109010, $2-3

Figurine, "I'm So Attached to You," 3.5", #109002, $2-3

Figurine, "You're My Bone-a-Fied Friend," 3.5", #108871, $2-3

Figurine, "You Put a Smile on My Face," 3", #108987, $2-3

Bottom markings on No Strings Attached figurine

Pamela Silin-Palmer

A decorative artist from the west coast, Pamela Silin-Palmer has created for Enesco a lovely line of ceramics and decorative accessories.

Pamela Silin-Palmer hang tag

Bottom markings on Pamela Silin-Palmer Canister

Pamela Silin-Palmer Teapot, $12-15

Pamela Silin-Palmer Canister Set, $20-25

Pandannas

Designed by Cindy Kurnicki, the "Fur-Ever Love" line of cold cast Pandanna figurines was issued in 1994.

Figurine, "Fur-Ever Tugging at My Heart," 3", #110582, $3-5

Figurine, "Fur-Ever My Treasure," 3", #110515, $3-5

Figurine, "Love Enough Fur Two," 3", #110604, $3-5

Figurine, "Showers of Love Fur You," 3.5", #107417, $3-5

Figurine, "All Wrapped Up in Love for You," 3", #110558, $3-5

Party Animals

Shown here is the Republican collection of Party Animals designed by Kathy Wise and issued in 1995.

Elephant Figurine, 4.5", #159883, $6-8

Elephant Figurine, 2", #159905, $4-6

Party Animal Pin, $3-4

Elephant Figurine, 3", 1995, $4-6

Elephant Figurine, 1.75", $4-6

Patterns of Life

Designed by Claudia Stenvig-Olsen and issued in 1997, these figurines are quite collectible.

December Quilt, "Joy," 3.5", #315044, $6-10

July Quilt, "Liberty," 3.5", #314986, $6-10

November Quilt, "Grace," 3.5", #315036, $6-10

To: ____________________

From: ____________________

The Angel Of July

July celebrates the red, white and blue,
With parades and fun just for you.
Unfurling the flag, such a grand sight.
Fireworks that sparkle and light up the night.
It's the pride of the angel named Liberty
With many smiles from sea to shining sea.

July Quilt pamphlet

Reverse side of November Quilt

October Quilt "Opal," 3.5", #315028, $6-10

Pennywhistle Lane

Introduced in 1994 and designed by Peter Fagan, these miniature cold cast figurines were patterned after antiques left in the attic by previous owners but are actually based on Peter Fagan's own personal collection. There is little demand for them on the secondary market.

Pennywhistle Lane pamphlet

Figurine, "Quiet Moments," 3.25", #655368, $1-2

Figurine, "Christmas Carol," 2", #655341, $1-2

Figurine, "Christmas Correspondent," 2", #655325, $1-2

Hanging Ornament, 2.25", #655422, $1-2

Pennywhistle Lane box

Figurine, "Santa Paws," 2", #655023, $1-2

Figurine, "Secret Presents," 1.5", #655430, $1-2

Figurine, "Pennywhistle Express," 1.5" high, 2" long, #655333, $1-2

Figurine, "Jack-in-the-Box," 2", #655449, $1-2

Figurine, "Passing Time," 4.75", #655414, $1-2

Figurine, "All I Want for Christmas," 2.25", #577618, $1-2

Figurine, "Trinkets Drum," 2.5", #655364, $1-2

Figurine, "James," 2.5", #655392, $1-2

Figurine, "Popsey," 2", #655376, $1-2

Figurine, "Juggling Jangles," 3.75", #655406, $1-2

Pretty as a Picture

Featuring figurines of endearing children, the Pretty as a Picture collection was designed by Kim Anderson and dates from the late 1990s.

Figurine, "We May Not Have it All Together but Together We Have it All," 4", #758469, *Courtesy of Kristen Gifford*, $6-10

Figurine, 5.25", #175331, *Courtesy of Kristen Gifford*, $6-10

Figurine, 4.5", #375934, *Courtesy of Kristen Gifford*, $6-10

Figurine, "Thanks to You I've Found Love," 4", #703435, *Courtesy of Kristen Gifford*, $6-10

Figurine, 3", #375926, *Courtesy of Kristen Gifford*, $6-10

Figurine, "A Rose for a Kiss, How Can I Miss," 4.75", #175307, *Courtesy of Kristen Gifford,* $6-10

Figurine, 5.5", #375594, *Courtesy of Kristen Gifford*, $6-10

Figurine, "You're My Winter Joy," 4.5", #375918, *Courtesy of Kristen Gifford*, $6-10

Figurine, "Let the Celebration Begin," 5", #247014, *Courtesy of Kristen Gifford*, $6-10

Sisters and Best Friends

Designed by Ellen Williams of Country Cousins fame, the Sisters and Best Friends figurines shown here date from 1994.

Sisters and Best Friends pamphlet

Recycling Figurine, "You Make the World a Better Place," 5", #772240, $6-8

Businesswoman Figurine, "You're the Image of Success," 5", #137154, $6-8

Double Figurine, "We're Champion Friends," 5.25", #772321, $6-8

Starlight Starbright

A charming Unicorn Collection of figurines from 1995, pleasing to collectors.

Figurine, "Follow Your Heart," 3", #153974, $5-7

Figurine, "Hang on to Your Dreams," 4", #153923, $5-7

Figurine, "Hitch Your Dreams to a Star," 4", #153966, $5-7

Bottom markings on Starlight Starbright figurine

Figurine, "Dreams Take Time," 3.5", #153893, $5-7

Tee-it-up

The Tee-it-up figurine collection is from 1992 by G & S Productions, Inc. and made to appeal to the golfing enthusiast. There is little demand for the figurines on the secondary market.

Tee It Up display

Figurine, 3.25", #718424, $1-2

Figurine, 3.25", #718343, $1-2

Figurine, 3.25", #718432, $1-2

Figurine, 3.25", #718262, $1-2

Figurine, 3.25", #718394, $1-2

Figurine, 3.5", #718270, $1-2

Figurine, 3.5", #718416, $1-2

Figurine, 3.5", #718254, $1-2

Figurine, 3.5", #718378, $1-2

Figurine, 3.5", #718304, $1-2

Figurine, 3.5", #718335, $1-2

Figurine, 3.5", #718327, $1-2

Figurine, 3.5", #718386, $1-2

Figurine, 3.5", #718408, $1-2

Figurine, 3.5", #718289, $1-2

Figurine, 3.5", #718315, $1-2

Figurine, 3.5", #718351, $1-2

Figurine, 3.5", #718297, $1-2

Titanic

The release of the move *Titanic* was the impetus for this collection of Titanic items from Enesco, which came out in 1998.

Salt and Pepper Shakers, #962643, $10-12

Night Light, #590053, $12-15

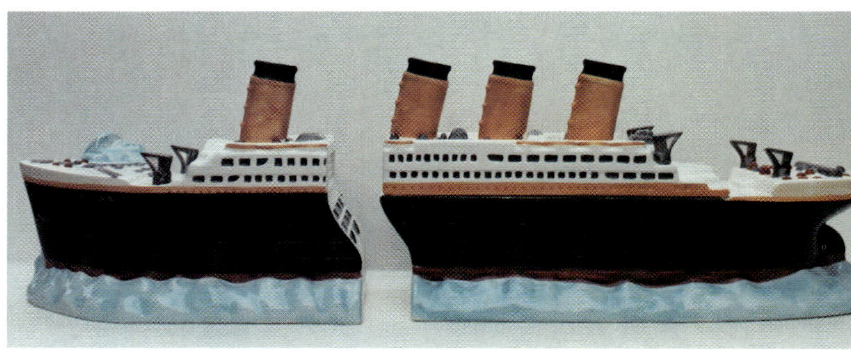

Cookie Jar, #962627, $20-25

Bank, #962635, $10-15

Titanic Cookie Jar box

Treasury of Christmas Ornaments

Enesco's line of Christmas ornaments was produced in one, two, or three year collectibles and called Treasury of Christmas.

Treasury of Christmas pamphlet

Ornament, McDonald's Collection 1992, "Twas the Night before Christmas," 3.5", #577545, $8-10

Ornament, "Casino Christmas" series, 6th Issue, "O Come All Ye Faithful," 2.25", #596280, $8-10

Ornament, General Mills 1991, "Christmas Cheer," 2.75", #585769, $8-10

Ornament, McDonald's Collection 1993, "A Quarter Pounder with Cheer," 2.25", #581569, $8-10

Ornament, Littlest Angel Series 1990, "Sweetest Greeting," 2.25", #830011, $8-10

Ornament, Baskin Robbins Series 1991, "Here's the Scoop," 2.5", #583693, $8-10

Ornament, Travelin' Santa Series 1990, "Bumper Car Santa," 3.5", #565083, $8-10

Ornament, For That Special Wife, "To My Gem," 3.25", $8-10

Ornament, Campbell's Series 1993, "Warm and Hearty Wishes," 3", #582344, $8-10

Chapter Four

Collectible Sets From Other Importing Companies

As an additional guide to identification, this chapter shows some of the figural ceramic sets prized by the collectors of today and imported from Japan in the 1950s, 1960s, and into the 1970s.

Lamb Set by Brinnco, *Courtesy of Jean Payne*

Cat Set by Royal Sealy, *Courtesy of Kim Lambert*

Prayer Girl Set by Giftcraft

Miss Priss Set by Lefton,
Courtesy of Jean Payne

Bluebird Set by Lefton,
Courtesy of Jean Payne

Dainty Miss Set by Lefton,
Courtesy of Jean Payne

Mr. Toodles Set by Lefton,
Courtesy of Jean Payne

Cabbage Girl by Lefton

Elf Set by Lefton

Big Eyes Set by Royal Sealy, *Courtesy of Jean Payne*

Miss Cutie Pie
Set by Napco

Whale Set by Norcrest

Papier Mache Pincushion and Cosmetic Holder Heads, *Courtesy of Kim Lambert*

Chef Set by Royal Sealy

Frog Family Set by Sears

Frog Family Canister Set by Sears

Frog Family Set by Sears

Mother-in-the-Kitchen Set by Sears,
Courtesy of Denise Dittner

Tulip Tyme Set by Shafford

Cat Set, unknown importer,
Courtesy of Jean Payne

Purple Cow Set, various importers,
Courtesy of Jean Payne

Dutch Girl and Boy Set, unknown importer

Dutch Girl Napkin Holder, unknown importer, *Courtesy of Denise Dittner*

Dutch Boy and Girl Sugar and Creamer, unknown importer, *Courtesy of Denise Dittner*

Chapter Five
Markings

Shown here are markings on the Enesco pieces found in this price guide.

Blue and silver label used in the 1950s and 1960s

Red and gold label, Japan, probably late 1960s and 1970s

Red and gold label, Taiwan, 1970s and 1980s

Black and gold Taiwan label, 1980s and 1990s

Red and gold butterfly label, Taiwan, 1980s and 1990s

Black and gold Korea label, 1980s and 1990s

Maruri Masterpiece Bone China imprint, late 1970s and 1980s

Red and gold crown label, found on bone china sets, 1960s and 1970s

Black and gold Sri Lanka label, 1980s and 1990s

More Schiffer Titles

www.schifferbooks.com

Josef Originals: Charming Figurines. Revised & Expanded 2nd Edition. Dee Harris, Jim and Kaye Whitaker. Ceramic figurines of beautiful and romantic young women were made in hundreds of different poses and costumes by Josef Originals. This all-color illustrated second edition follows the art of California ceramicist Mauriel Josef George from 1945 through the 1980s. Packed with hundreds of cheerful images, this book will be an invaluable aid in the dating and identification of these abundant figurines.
Size: 8 1/2" x 11" 574 photos 128pp.
Price Guide/Index
ISBN: 0-7643-0886-6 soft cover $24.95

Napco®. Kathleen Deel. Ceramic pieces sold by Napco® (National Potteries Corporation) are distinctive and popular again today. From its prolific output of the 1950s and 1960s to its miniature bone china imports of the 1970s, Napco has held the interest of collectors because the ceramic items are consistently well-designed. This volume brings together information on all of the Napco™ lines, including chapters on animal figures, birthday sets, decorative items and kitchenware, figurines and planters, and head vases. There is a separate section on Inarco™ (International Artware Corporation), sister company of Napco. Collectors of holiday items, angels, and nursery rhyme characters will find plenty of interest in these pages. An added bonus is the directory of major importing companies of the fifties and sixties. With over 1,000 color photos and a price guide, this is a worthwhile addition to a ceramics collector's library.
Size: 8 1/2" x 11" 1,164 color photos 182pp.
Price Guide
ISBN: 0-7643-0844-0 soft cover $29.95

The Encyclopedia of Head Vases. Kathleen Cole. Head vases, developed for the florist industry in the twentieth century, and now an increasingly popular collectible, were made in a variety of sizes and styles. The Encyclopedia of Head Vases provides a broad perspective on vases available, placing special emphasis on those heads which had not previously been pictured in a book.Almost 1,000 color photographs and captions identifying size and marks of 1309 heads make identification easy. Special chapters on the popular Betty Lou Nichols heads, Christmas heads, wall pockets, and related collectibles, along with a current price guide will make this book and important reference for collectors and dealers.
Size: 8 1/2" x 11" 976 color photos 208pp.
Price Guide
ISBN: 0-88740-928-8 hard cover $29.95

Lady Head Vases. Revised. Mary Zavada. A new and quickly popularized field of collectibles is lady head vases which were manufactured in the 1950's to the middle 1960's and sold by florists. the vases for the most part were made of semi-porcelain and the vast majority were produced in Japan, but occasionally one marked USA can be found. This book has over 300 charming lady head vases illustrated in color. Collecting tips and a price guide are also included.
Size: 9" x 6" Over 300 vases illustrated 112pp.
Price Guide
ISBN: 0-88740-880-X soft cover $16.95

Figural Planters. Kathleen Deel. If you love collecting and are looking for a new collectible, this book is for you! Pictured are hundreds of planters imported since the 1950s, mainly for use by the floral industry. From lovely ladies in brightly colored Christmas and Valentine dresses to little boys playing baseball, there is something for everyone in this book. A large section is devoted to baby vases, as well as nursery rhyme characters and loveable Raggedy Ann and Andys. The accumulation of several years of extensive searching by the author, the book does justice to the amazing variety and ingenious design of these planters. Separated into specific categories with many lovely examples of each type of vase illustrated, this book will take you on an extended journey into the world of imported figural planters.
Size: 6" x 9" 375+ color photos 160pp.
Price Guide
ISBN: 0-88740-970-9 soft cover $19.95

Snow Babies, Santas, and Elves: Collecting Christmas Bisque Figures. Mary Morrison. Snow babies appeal not only to Christmas enthusiasts, but to collectors of dolls, figurines, and miniatures. Principally manufactured in Germany in the early part of this century, these tiny grouted figures decorated cakes in England and mantel pieces in the United States. Today they are avidly sought by collectors, who still use them to create little winter scenes.This carefully researched and documented book explores the origins of snow babies. (Were they created to honor Marie Peary, the daughter of Admiral Peary and the first white baby born in Northern Greenland?) The collection of 700 color photographs, the largest ever published, displays exquisite all-white pieces and the smaller action snow babies. It also introduces the reader to the rare blue and pink snow pieces. Included are chapters on bisque Santas (over 150 of them), elves, dwarves, snowmen, buildings, animals, and other pieces that are collected and displayed with snow babies. A rarity scale and price guide are included.
Size: 8 1/2" x 11" 693 color photos 160pp.
Price Guide
ISBN: 0-88740-493-6 soft cover $29.95